Bloggers across the country have fallen in love with

4 Ingredients

"If you want to add some simplicity to the kitchen without sacrificing good taste, then check out *4 Ingredients.*"
—*My Sentiment Exactly*

"Four ingredients might not sound glamorous, but look at some of the dishes: Antipasto Tarts, Carrot & Cilantro Soup, Apricot Chicken, Tandoori Lamb, and Orange & Almond Cake . . . hot diggity simple cookin' dog."
—*Mom Most Traveled*

"Their mantra of 'keep it simple' is totally my style and a concept I can appreciate."
—*Simply Being Mommy*

"If you like to cook but want simplicity in your already chaotic life, I urge you to check out this book!"
—*West Michigan Mommy*

"This cookbook is a must have in my cupboard!"
—*Minnesota Mama's Must Haves*

"This cookbook has so many fun recipes, each using 4 ingredients or less, and minimal measuring and mess!"
—*What Mama Wants*

"This is a must-have cookbook for any busy family."
—*Mommy Living the Life of Riley*

"This is quickly becoming a staple in my kitchen."
—*Mom on the Random*

"And the best part? Oh, that's easy. Being able to put something amazing on the dinner table and not having to break the bank buying ingredients!"
—*Misadventures in Baby Raising*

"This book is a wonderful source of inspiration but also that clean slate so many of us are looking for in preparing family meals."
—*ModernMom.com*

Also by Kim McCosker and Rachael Bermingham

4 Ingredients

Ingredients
Gluten-Free

More Than 400 New and Exciting Recipes All Made
with 4 or Fewer Ingredients and All Gluten-Free!

. . . .

Kim McCosker and Rachael Bermingham

ATRIA PAPERBACK

New York   London   Toronto   Sydney   New Delhi

ATRIA PAPERBACK
A Division of Simon & Schuster, Inc.
1230 Avenue of the Americas
New York, NY 10020

First Atria Paperback edition March 2012

ATRIA PAPERBACK and colophon are trademarks of Simon & Schuster, Inc.

For information about special discounts for bulk purchases, please contact Simon & Schuster Special Sales at 1-866-506-1949 or business@simonandschuster.com.

The Simon & Schuster Speakers Bureau can bring authors to your live event. For more information or to book an event, contact the Simon & Schuster Speakers Bureau at 1-866-248-3049 or visit our website at www.simonspeakers.com.

Manufactured in the United States of America

10   9   8   7   6   5   4   3   2

Library of Congress Cataloging-in-Publication Data

McCosker, Kim.
4 ingredients gluten-free : more than 400 new and exciting recipes all made with 4 or fewer ingredients and all gluten-free! / Kim McCosker, Rachael Bermingham
     p. cm.
1. Gluten-free diet—Recipes. 2. Cookbooks.
I. Bermingham, Rachael. II. Title. III. Title: Four ingredients gluten-free.
RM237.86.M377   2012
641.3—dc23   2011051256

ISBN 978-1-4516-3571-3
ISBN 978-1-4516-3573-7 (ebook)

CONTENTS

FOREWORD

Since we started our *4 Ingredients* journey back in 2007, with the Australian publication of our first book, we have done hundreds of appearances and book signings and have met literally thousands of fabulous people from all over the world. At these events, one of the most common questions we were asked was, "Do you have any gluten-free recipes?" And the answer was, in fact, "YES, we have *hundreds* of absolutely gorgeous gluten-free recipes!"

We had dabbled a *little* with gluten-free cooking (Rach's husband, Paul, has an intolerance). However, it wasn't until we continued to receive this question so frequently that we considered doing a book dedicated to those who are completely gluten intolerant.

As we started researching, we were *astounded* to see statistics showing that one in one hundred Australians most likely has celiac disease. How many people are still undiagnosed? And that's just in our native Australia. What would the global count come to? Surprisingly, what we also discovered was that there are a large number of people who just want to cut back on wheat, rye, oats, and barley in their everyday diets, choosing to do so not because of intolerance to gluten but purely as a lifestyle choice.

Initially we thought creating recipes would be a mammoth task, when you consider that gluten is found in so many ingredients. It's in many flavored commercial spreads and sauces, some hams, almost all packaged cookies and crackers, some sausages, packaged sauce and soup mixes, most cake mixes, common breads, tortillas, confectioners' sugar, and a whole lot more. Compiling this book has required a huge learning curve, and it's also been incredibly satisfying to rise to the challenge of substituting gluten-free flours for normal flours and coming up with delicious dishes that anyone—celiac sufferer or not—will enjoy. As with all things, if you seek, you shall find; if you ask, you shall receive an answer; and if you persist, it will happen!

We would like to take this opportunity to thank our always supportive husbands, families, and friends, as well as Graham, Cheryl, and the team at The Coeliac Society of Australia, which has been an invaluable source of information and guidance while we were compiling this book.

4 Ingredients Gluten-Free, with over 400 simple, speedy, and scrumptious recipes, is proof that a gluten-free lifestyle can be delicious!

Best wishes and happy cooking!

Kim and Rachael

WARNING!

In an effort to make this book as user-friendly as possible, and to help you when you're shopping, we chose to list the ingredients that we used in many of our recipes.

These ingredients at the time of writing were endorsed by The Coeliac Society of Australia as being gluten-free. And many of them have "gluten-free" clearly marked on them.

However, changes may happen. Manufacturing processes change, ingredients change, labels change.

As a precaution, ALWAYS check the labels for updated information and warnings to ensure that what you think you are eating is what you are actually eating!

WHAT IS GLUTEN?

Gluten is a protein found in grains, including wheat, rye, oats, and barley. Gluten is found in some soups, some mayonnaises, and many processed foods, as well as in wheat starch binders and fillers. Gluten can also be found in medications and in some vitamins.

People with celiac disease are sensitive to gluten, which damages the lining of the small bowel. This damage can lead to symptoms including fatigue, anemia, irritable bowel–type symptoms, and vitamin and mineral deficiencies.

When you are choosing products, it is very important to check the ingredient listing.

We highly recommend the following websites for more information:

Association of European Coeliac Societies: www.aoecs.org
Celiac.com: www.celiac.com
Celiac Disease Center at Columbia University: www.celiacdiseasecenter
.columbia.edu
Celiac Disease Foundation: www.celiac.org
The Coeliac Society of Australia: www.coeliacsociety.com.au
National Foundation for Celiac Awareness: www.celiaccentral.org

GLUTEN FOODS

DID YOU KNOW?

As written in the book *Gluten-Free Baking with the Culinary Institute of America*:

"Coeliac" is a Greek word referring to the abdomen and was first referenced by the Greek physician Araetaeus of Cappadocia, during the first or second century A.D. But it wasn't until after the Dutch famine of WWII, when wheat flour was scarce, that the connection between celiac disease and the ingestion of wheat was made. A Dutch pediatrician, Willem Karel Dicke, made the connection in 1950!

Here is a helpful table supplied to us by the The Coeliac Society of Australia of foods that are good for a gluten-free diet and foods that are not.

FOODS TO AVOID (contain gluten)	FOODS TO INCLUDE (gluten-free)
Barley	Amaranth flour
Beer (unless gluten-free)	Arrowroot
Oatmeal	Buckwheat flour
Pearl barley	Carob
Rye	Chickpea flour (also called besan)
Triticale	Coconut flour
Wheat bran	Corn flour, cornmeal, polenta
Wheat flour: all-purpose, atta, farina, graham, self-rising, semolina, whole wheat	Cream of rice
	Gluten-free flour mixes
	Lentil flour
Wheat forms: bulghur (bulgur, burghul, bulgar), cracked wheat, wheat berries, wheat germ	Lupin flour
	Millet
	Potato flour
Wheat varieties: dinkel, durum, emmer, farro, kamut, spelt	Quinoa
	Rice (all varieties including glutinous)
	Rice flour / rice bran
	Sago
	Sorghum
	Soy: flour, beans
	Tapioca
	Teff

IN THE CUPBOARD

As we did in *4 Ingredients*, we have suggested a list of ingredients that you may want to stock up on to help create the wonderful meals and treats found in the following pages. All the items on the list may be found in gluten-free stores, in organic supermarkets, and often in your local supermarkets. If you can't find an item, don't be afraid to ask the store manager to order it for you.

Please note: We have not included salt, pepper, and water as part of the 4 Ingredients.

SAVORY
Cold-pressed extra virgin macadamia nut oil
Extra virgin macadamia oil spray
Free-range eggs
Fresh vegetables
Garlic
Ginger
Gluten-free basil pesto
Gluten-free barbecue sauce
Gluten-free bread crumbs
Gluten-free cornstarch
Gluten-free curry powder
Gluten-free Dijon mustard
Gluten-free flour: all-purpose and self-rising
Gluten-free mayonnaise

Gluten-free soy sauce
Gluten-free pasta
Gluten-free stocks
Gluten-free vegetable seasoning
Gluten-free Worcestershire sauce
Gluten-free ketchup
Lemons
Peppercorns
Pine nuts
Rice
Sea salt
Sesame seeds
Sour cream
Vinegar (but not malt vinegar)
SWEET
Cinnamon
Condensed milk
Cream
Cream cheese
Coconut, shredded
Evaporated milk
Fruit: canned, dried, fresh
Honey
Jams: apricot, strawberry, marmalade, etc.
Nutmeg
Spice blends
Sugar: raw, brown, granulated, superfine
Vanilla extract

HEALTHY FOOD SUBSTITUTES

We are blessed with being different and special in our own right, and that also goes for the ways our bodies operate. The one thing we all have in common is the essential requirement for loads of nutrients to keep our bodies functioning at their optimal levels.

A terrific way to satisfy the body's basic nutritional requirements is to eat more organic or home-grown products, which we use wherever possible. Not only are these full to the brim with a fabulous array of nutrients, but they are incredibly delicious.

However, not everyone can readily access these products. We did not include these in our recipes, opting instead to add this section, which we feel is vital to your and your family's health. For information regarding organic foods, we recommend our good friend Cyndi O'Meara's book *Changing Habits, Changing Lives.*

PRODUCT	SUBSTITUTE
White sugar	Brown sugar
	Organic raw sugar*
Oil	Avocado oil
	Cold-pressed extra virgin olive oil*
	Cold-pressed macadamia nut oil*
	Grapeseed oil
Cooking spray	Cold-pressed macadamia nut oil *
Flour, wheat	Gluten-free all-purpose flour *
	Gluten-free self-rising flour *
	Rice flour *
Margarine	Butter*

PRODUCT	SUBSTITUTE
Eggs	Free-range eggs*
Milk	Organic milk*
	Raw milk (pasteurized only)
Pasta	Gluten-free pasta*
Honey	Organic honey*
Jams	Homemade jams made from raw ingredients
	Organic jam*
Soy sauce	Gluten-free soy sauce*

*Where possible, buy products labeled "certified organic," as these products have passed all the stringent tests to ensure that they really are organic and therefore are loaded with nutrients and flavor.

YUMMY CONDIMENTS & DIPS

If in doubt, leave it out. If there's no doubt, you can pig out!

—Graham Price, The Coeliac Society of Australia

Artichoke Dip

SERVES 4 TO 6

Serve with a platter of fresh vegetable sticks: pepper, radish, carrot, celery, etc.

⅔ cup olive oil

1 jar (6.5 ounces) marinated artichokes, drained

¾ cup grated Parmesan cheese

1 clove garlic

In a blender, combine all the ingredients and process until nice and smooth. Season with sea salt and pepper to taste.

Avo & Corn Dip

SERVES 6

A recipe from Jules Boag that's delicious served with veggie sticks.

3 ripe avocados

2 tablespoons sour cream

¼ cup canned GF creamed corn

¼ teaspoon cayenne pepper

Mash and mix all the ingredients together.

Balsamic Vinaigrette

MAKES 1 CUP

¼ cup balsamic vinegar

1 tablespoon GF Dijon mustard

¾ cup extra virgin olive oil

In a medium bowl, whisk together the vinegar and mustard. Slowly pour in the olive oil, whisking constantly until combined. Season with sea salt and pepper to taste.

NOTE: Vinaigrette will keep in an airtight container in the fridge for up to 1 week. Whisk to combine just before serving.

Basil Dip

SERVES 4

Easy and ultra tasty! Recipe by Laurent Vancam.

1 large bunch basil, leaves and stems

2 cloves garlic, crushed

1 cup grated Parmesan cheese

¼ cup olive oil

In a blender, combine all the ingredients and process until smooth.

Basil Pesto

MAKES 1 CUP

½ cup pine nuts

1 cup grated Parmesan cheese

1 large bunch basil, leaves and stems

1 tablespoon olive oil

In an ungreased skillet, toast ¼ cup of the pine nuts. Combine all the pine nuts, the Parmesan, and the basil in a blender and blitz. Mix with the olive oil.

OPTIONAL: Alter the flavor by adding a drop or two of lemon juice and 1 clove garlic.

Blue Cheese Dressing

MAKES 1 CUP

1 ounce blue cheese

⅓ cup GF mayonnaise

⅓ cup plain yogurt

3 tablespoons chopped chives

Use a fork to mash the blue cheese in a small bowl. Add the remaining ingredients and mix well. Season with pepper to taste.

SERVING SUGGESTION: This is a lovely dressing on a baked potato or on your favorite burger, pizza base, or salad.

Butter Bean & Mustard Topper

SERVES 4 TO 6

Serve on GF crackers.

1 can (15 ounces) butter beans, rinsed and drained

1 teaspoon GF whole-grain or GF Dijon mustard

3 tablespoons olive oil

2 tablespoons finely chopped flat-leaf parsley

In a blender, combine the beans and mustard. With the blender running, add the olive oil and blend until smooth. You will probably need to add a little water to get the desired consistency. Add the parsley and black pepper to taste.

NOTE: Parsley is the world's most popular herb. It contains three times as much vitamin C as oranges and twice as much iron as spinach; is rich in vitamin A; and contains folate, potassium, and calcium.

Caramelized Balsamic Vinegar

MAKES 1 CUP

1 cup balsamic vinegar

¼ cup packed light brown sugar

In a small saucepan, combine the vinegar and brown sugar and bring to a boil over low heat. Stir until the sugar dissolves. Boil for 1 minute, then reduce the heat and stir until the mixture caramelizes and darkens. Let cool, and store in the refrigerator.

SERVING SUGGESTION: This is beautiful served over sweet *and* savory. It's especially good with Bite-Size Fried Haloumi (page 42).

Caramel Sauce

MAKES 2 CUPS

This is heaven served over just about anything!

1 cup heavy cream

¾ cup packed light brown sugar

8 tablespoons (1 stick) unsalted butter

In a small saucepan, combine all the ingredients and bring to a boil over medium heat. Simmer for 2 minutes.

Cashew Cream

MAKES 1 CUP

A recipe from Kim Morrison, who says, "This makes a delicious change from cream on cakes, pancakes, and desserts!"

4 ounces unsalted raw cashew nuts

3 oranges, peeled and chopped

1 apple, peeled

1 tablespoon honey

In a blender, combine all the ingredients and process until smooth and creamy. Serve chilled.

Cinnamon Dip

MAKES 1 CUP

Serve with a platter of fresh fruit and dried apricots for dipping.

1 cup sour cream

3 generous teaspoons GF ground cinnamon

1 tablespoon light brown sugar

In a small bowl, combine all the ingredients and mix well. Chill for at least 2 hours before serving, to let the flavors develop.

Classic Salad Dressing

MAKES ½ CUP

2 tablespoons fresh lemon juice

¼ cup extra virgin olive oil

1 teaspoon GF Dijon mustard

½ clove garlic, crushed through a press

In a screw-top jar, combine all the ingredients plus sea salt and pepper to taste. Shake well.

NOTE: When a jar of mustard is nearly empty, add some olive oil and wine vinegar and shake well for a delicious salad dressing.

Corn Relish & Bacon Dip

MAKES 2 CUPS

This is D.E.L.I.S.H! Serve with your favorite GF crackers.

5 slices bacon, chopped

1 cup GF corn relish

1¼ cups sour cream

¼ cup chopped scallions

In a nonstick skillet, cook the bacon over medium heat until nice and crispy. Drain on paper towels and blot off any excess fat. Transfer to a bowl to cool. Stir in the remaining ingredients. Refrigerate for 30 minutes before serving.

Cranberry Compote

MAKES 1 CUP

Serve with turkey or chicken, or as a dipping sauce to accompany a cheese platter.

1 yellow onion, chopped

½ cup dried cranberries

2 tablespoons light brown sugar

⅓ cup balsamic vinegar

In a saucepan, cook the onion in 2 tablespoons water until softened. Add the cranberries, brown sugar, and vinegar. Simmer until caramelized.

Cumin Aioli

MAKES 1 CUP

1 cup GF mayonnaise

2 tablespoons GF Dijon
mustard

1 clove garlic, crushed

1 tablespoon ground cumin

Mix all the ingredients together and chill
for at least 30 minutes to give the flavors
time to develop.

SERVING SUGGESTION: This is a really nice accompaniment to
Sweet Potato Fries (page 242; omit the cinnamon sugar), Chicken
& Chorizo Skewers (page 42), and grilled fish.

Date, Pistachio, Orange & Mint Salsa

SERVES 4

*A recipe from the lovely Marie McColl. This makes a delicious
salsa to serve with grilled lamb or pork. Or omit the dates and
serve it atop a piece of your favorite grilled fish.*

4 ounces dates, pitted and
chopped

2 tablespoons chopped
pistachio nuts

4 sprigs mint, chopped

2 oranges, peeled and
cubed

Combine all the ingredients.

Easy Hummus

MAKES 1 CUP

Serve with vegetable sticks and GF crackers.

1 can (15 ounces) chickpeas (garbanzo beans), drained, liquid reserved

1 clove garlic, crushed

2 teaspoons ground cumin

1 tablespoon olive oil

In a blender or food processor, combine all the ingredients with ½ teaspoon sea salt. Blend at low speed, gradually adding the reserved bean liquid until the desired consistency is reached.

Easy Mocha Sauce

MAKES 2 CUPS

Serve this with poached pears—simply stunning!

7 ounces dark chocolate

1¼ cups heavy cream

2 teaspoons instant coffee

In a microwaveable bowl, combine all the ingredients and microwave for 2 minutes, stopping to stir every 30 seconds.

Feta Dip

MAKES 1 CUP

This is really, really tasty. Serve with fresh veggie sticks or your favorite GF crackers.

8 ounces feta cheese

¼ cup olive oil

1 clove garlic, crushed

¼ cup milk

In a food processor, combine the feta, oil, and garlic and blend. With the machine running, gradually add the milk in a slow stream and process until smooth. Chill before serving.

Garlic Butter

MAKES ½ CUP

4 tablespoons (½ stick) butter, at room temperature

1 clove garlic, crushed through a press

1 teaspoon fresh lemon juice

1 teaspoon finely chopped parsley

Combine all the ingredients. Season with sea salt and pepper to taste.

Garlic Cream Sauce

MAKES 1 CUP

Dollop this onto the top of your favorite steak.

1 teaspoon extra virgin olive oil

1 clove garlic, crushed through a press

1½ tablespoons GF Worcestershire sauce

6 tablespoons heavy cream

In a nonstick skillet, heat the oil. Add the garlic and cook until fragrant. Stir in the Worcestershire sauce and cream and heat through.

Greek Yogurt & Mayonnaise

MAKES 1 CUP

This is absolutely sensational and will make a salad eater of anyone! Make sure to choose a mayonnaise made with real eggs.

½ cup plain Greek yogurt

½ cup GF mayonnaise

Mix well and serve over salad.

Grilled Cheese Salsa Dip

MAKES 1 CUP

A Mexicana marvel . . . too easy and too tasty! Serve with vegetable sticks and GF corn chips. Mmmmmm!

8 ounces Edam or Gouda cheese, grated

2 tablespoons light cream

½ cup chunky tomato salsa

In a small saucepan, melt the Edam or Gouda over medium-low heat. Stir in the cream, stirring frequently to keep the cheese from burning. Transfer to a warmed serving dish and top with the salsa.

Guacamole

SERVES 4

Serve with GF corn chips.

1 ripe avocado

1 small tomato, finely chopped

½ bunch cilantro, chopped

1 tablespoon fresh lime juice

Halve and pit the avocado. Scoop the flesh into a bowl and mash. Mix in the tomato, cilantro, lime juice, and sea salt and pepper to taste. Chill before serving.

OPTIONAL: Add a little finely chopped Spanish onion.

NOTE: Prepare ahead of time and put the avocado pit back into the dip to help prevent discoloration.

Hollandaise Sauce

MAKES 1 CUP

3 egg yolks

8 tablespoons (1 stick) butter, melted

2 tablespoons white wine vinegar or fresh lemon juice

In a bowl, with an electric mixer, beat the egg yolks for 10 minutes, or until pale and thick. With the mixer running, gradually add the melted butter. Mix in the vinegar. Season with sea salt and pepper to taste.

OPTIONAL: Add tarragon for béarnaise sauce.

Hot Fudge Sauce

MAKES 1 CUP

You'll wish you'd made more! Serve drizzled over a banana split, ice cream and berries, or Peanut Butter Ice Cream Pie (page 187) . . . oooh la la!

7 ounces semisweet chocolate, chopped

1 cup chopped GF marshmallows

1 cup heavy cream

In a microwaveable bowl, combine all the ingredients. Microwave on high in 30-second increments, stirring until nice and smooth.

Lemon Aioli

MAKES ½ CUP

Works well with almost any fish dish!

½ cup GF mayonnaise

1 clove garlic, crushed through a press

2 tablespoons fresh lemon juice, plus a little grated lemon zest, if desired

Combine all the ingredients. Season with sea salt and pepper to taste. Chill for several hours before serving.

Lemon & Olive Oil Dressing

MAKES ¼ CUP

2 tablespoons fresh lemon juice

¼ cup olive oil

Combine the ingredients and mix well. Season with sea salt and pepper to taste.

SERVING SUGGESTION: This is lovely served over fresh salad greens.

Lemon Butter

MAKES 2 CUPS

A recipe by Liz Woodcraft.

8 tablespoons (1 stick) butter

1½ cups sugar

6 eggs

3 large lemons

In a microwaveable bowl, combine the butter and sugar. Microwave until the butter melts. In a separate bowl, beat the eggs until frothy. Finely grate the zest of 1 lemon, then juice all 3 lemons. Add the lemon juice, lemon zest, and beaten eggs to the butter-sugar mixture. Microwave on medium-high in 1-minute increments, stirring after each, for 5 minutes.

Mayonnaise

MAKES 1½ CUPS

1 egg

2 teaspoons white wine vinegar

½ teaspoon sea salt

1¼ cups sunflower oil

In a food processor, combine the egg, vinegar, and sea salt. With the machine running, gradually pour in the oil. The longer you leave the machine on, the thicker the mayonnaise will get. Store in the refrigerator for 3 to 4 days in an airtight container.

OPTIONAL: Add 1 teaspoon GF Dijon mustard.

NOTE: Homemade mayonnaise does contain raw egg yolks, so there is the possibility of salmonella bacteria. To reduce the risk, keep well chilled.

Mint Glaze

MAKES ENOUGH TO GLAZE A ROAST

Serve roast lamb with this glaze.

1 tablespoon finely chopped mint

1 tablespoon fresh lemon juice

1 tablespoon sugar

1 tablespoon boiling water

In a small saucepan, combine all the ingredients and cook over low heat for 5 minutes. Let stand for 30 minutes before serving.

Mushroom Sauce

MAKES 2 CUPS

*Rach's #1 favorite!! Serve with your favorite steak
or some grilled chicken.*

4 tablespoons (½ stick) butter

2 cups sliced mushrooms

1 GF beef bouillon cube mixed with ½ cup hot water

¾ cup heavy cream

In a nonstick skillet, melt the butter. Add the mushrooms and cook for 3 to 5 minutes, or until soft. Add the beef stock and cream and simmer until the sauce thickens slightly.

Orange & Mustard Dressing

MAKES ABOUT ½ CUP

¼ cup orange juice

2 tablespoons balsamic vinegar

1 tablespoon GF whole-grain mustard

2 teaspoons honey

Whisk all the ingredients together. Season with sea salt and pepper to taste.

Oyster Dip

MAKES 1 CUP

Scrumptious served with fresh carrot sticks or GF crackers.

2 cans (3.75 ounces each) smoked oysters, drained

8 ounces reduced-fat cream cheese

2 lemons, juiced

Pinch cayenne pepper

Put all the ingredients, with a pinch of sea salt, into a blender and whiz until smooth. Transfer to a bowl and serve.

Peps Dressing

MAKES ABOUT ¼ CUP

Recipe by Lea Van Dijk.

3 tablespoons extra virgin olive oil

2 tablespoons white wine vinegar

1 teaspoon GF whole-grain mustard

In a screw-top jar, combine all the ingredients, plus pepper to taste. Shake well.

Quick Fire Chutney

MAKES 2 CUPS

Recipe by Chef Dan Primmer. This is sensational served over grilled chicken or pork and a great way to use those overripe pears!

½ red onion, chopped into chunks

2 pears, chopped into chunks

2 tablespoons light brown sugar

1½ teaspoons chopped fresh mint

In a nonstick skillet, cook the onion in a little water for 2 minutes to soften. Add the pears and cook until they soften. Add ¼ cup water and the brown sugar, reduce the heat to low, and simmer until the liquid reduces. Remove from the heat and let cool before gently stirring in the mint.

Raita

MAKES 2 CUPS

This is the perfect accompaniment for hot and spicy dishes, as the yogurt cuts the heat!

1 cup plain Greek yogurt

1 small cucumber, finely chopped

1 tablespoon chopped fresh mint

1 small vine-ripened tomato, diced

Mix all the ingredients together. Season well with sea salt and pepper.

Raspberry Sauce

MAKES ½ CUP

Delicious drizzled over ice cream or swirled through cheesecakes (see Cheesecake Fillings, pages 172 and 173).

4 ounces raspberries

2 tablespoons GF confectioners' sugar

2 teaspoons orange juice

In a blender, combine all the ingredients and process until smooth. Strain to remove the seeds.

Roasted Eggplant Dip

MAKES 1 CUP

2 large eggplants, sliced

Juice of 1 lemon

1 clove garlic, crushed through a press

2 tablespoons tahini

Preheat the oven to 350°F. Line a baking sheet with parchment paper. Place the eggplants on the baking sheet and bake for 30 minutes, or until very soft. When cool, peel off the skin and discard. Transfer the flesh to a bowl and stir in the remaining ingredients. Refrigerate for 1 hour before serving to let the flavors blend.

OPTIONAL: Serve sprinkled with paprika and fresh parsley.

Roquefort & Peppercorn Sauce

SERVES 4

1 cup heavy cream

3 to 4 ounces Roquefort cheese, crumbled

2 to 3 tablespoons mixed peppercorns

1 tablespoon chopped flat-leaf parsley

In a large saucepan, heat the cream until it's just about to boil. Simmer for 1 to 2 minutes, then lower the heat and add the Roquefort. With a rolling pin, lightly crush the peppercorns, then add them to the cream and cheese mixture and stir to combine. Cook over medium heat, stirring, for 3 to 4 minutes, so that the sauce thickens and the flavors meld. Add sea salt if desired. Serve over beef, pork, or chicken, and garnish with the chopped parsley.

Salsa

MAKES 1 CUP

Serve over grilled pork . . . YUM!

1 avocado, diced

1 teaspoon finely chopped red chile pepper

Juice of ½ lime

¼ red bell pepper, diced

Combine all the ingredients.

Satay Sauce

MAKES 3 CUPS

Recipe by Chef Dan Primmer.
This is delicious over kebabs and dolloped on top of
Sweet Potato Fries (page 242; omit the cinnamon sugar).

1 onion, diced

2 cups coconut cream

1 cup crunchy peanut butter

4 sprigs cilantro, chopped

In a nonstick skillet, cook the onion in a little water until translucent. Stir in the coconut cream and peanut butter and stir over low heat until combined and warmed through. Stir in the cilantro.

Tapenade

MAKES ½ CUP

Serve with fresh veggie sticks or GF crackers.

⅔ cup kalamata olives, pitted

1 clove garlic, crushed

2 tablespoons torn basil leaves

1½ tablespoons olive oil

In a blender, combine all the ingredients and process until smooth. Cover and refrigerate until ready to serve.

Tartar Sauce

MAKES ¾ CUP

Recipe by Brett McCosker.

½ cup plain yogurt

1 tablespoon drained capers, chopped

2 gherkins, finely chopped

1 tablespoon finely chopped flat-leaf parsley

Combine all the ingredients. Serve chilled.

Tempura Batter

MAKES 2 CUPS

Use with small-cut vegetables and meats and shallow-fry.

1¼ cups GF cornstarch

1¼ cups ice-cold seltzer or club soda

Sift the cornstarch into a bowl and add a pinch of sea salt. Make a well in the center and add the seltzer, mixing until smooth and lump-free. Set aside for 10 to 15 minutes before using.

Thai Dressing

MAKES ½ CUP

2 tablespoons sugar

2 tablespoons fresh lime juice

⅓ cup fish sauce

GF chili powder to taste

In a screw-top jar, combine all the ingredients. Shake well.

Vinaigrette

MAKES 1 CUP

½ cup olive oil

½ cup white wine vinegar

4 to 6 sprigs flat-leaf parsley, finely chopped

2 teaspoons GF Dijon mustard

In a screw-top jar, combine all the ingredients. Shake well.

Warm Cheese Dip

MAKES 2 CUPS

This is R.e.a.l.l.y Y.u.m.m.y!! Serve with GF crackers and fresh veggie sticks.

2 tablespoons butter

½ teaspoon ground cumin

1 cup sour cream

2 cups grated Cheddar cheese

In a medium saucepan, melt the butter over low heat. Add the cumin and stir for 1 minute. Add the sour cream and when warm, add the Cheddar. Stir constantly until the cheese melts and the mixture is smooth. Serve warm.

Wasabi Dressing

MAKES 1 CUP

2 teaspoons GF wasabi paste

⅓ cup fresh lemon juice

⅓ cup peanut oil

2 teaspoons finely chopped cilantro

In a screw-top jar, combine all the ingredients. Shake well.

OPTIONAL: For extra flavor, substitute 2 tablespoons sesame oil and 1 tablespoon peanut oil for the ⅓ cup peanut oil.

White Sauce

MAKES 1 CUP

2 tablespoons butter

2 tablespoons GF all-purpose flour

1 cup milk

In a saucepan, melt the butter, then remove from the heat. Stir in the flour and blend in the milk. Return to the heat and stir until the sauce boils and thickens, then simmer for 2 minutes. Season with sea salt and pepper to taste. Add more milk if a thinner sauce is desired.

OPTIONAL: This is delicious flavored with orange zest and chopped parsley; serve it over corned beef. Or use it with Parmesan cheese for lasagna.

BREAKFASTS

All happiness depends on a leisurely breakfast.

—John Gunther

Almond Muffins

MAKES 12

You will be surprised at how quick and easy these are.

¾ cup GF self-rising flour, sifted

¼ cup almond meal

3 tablespoons sugar

1¼ cups heavy cream

Preheat the oven to 350°F. Grease a 12-cup mini muffin tin or use nonstick. In a bowl, mix all the ingredients until just combined. Spoon the batter into the muffin cups. Bake for 20 minutes, or until golden brown.

OPTIONAL: Add fresh blueberries or raspberries or whatever fruit you have to the mix.

Almond Pancakes

MAKES 12

3 eggs

1 cup almond meal

½ cup Greek yogurt

2 tablespoons butter

In a bowl, whisk the eggs. Add the almond meal and enough yogurt to form a batter. In a small nonstick skillet, heat the butter over medium-high heat. For each pancake, pour in a little of the batter and cook for 1 to 2 minutes, or until it begins to set. Flip gently and cook on the second side.

OPTIONAL: Delicious served with a dollop of yogurt and a sprinkling of brown sugar.

Apple Fritters

MAKES 6

1 slice GF bread, grated

1 teaspoon cinnamon sugar

1 egg

1 apple, grated

In a bowl, combine the bread, cinnamon sugar, egg, and 1 tablespoon water and mix well. Stir in the apple. Drop the batter by tablespoons into a hot nonstick skillet. Cook until golden on the bottom, then flip gently and cook on the other side until golden brown.

Baked Raspberry French Toast

SERVES 6

A deliciously different way to prepare French toast.

¾ cup raspberry jam

12 slices GF bread, crusts removed

6 eggs

1 cup milk

Preheat the oven to 375°F. Generously grease an 11 by 7-inch baking dish. Spread jam on 6 slices of the bread. Top with the remaining bread to form 6 sandwiches. Beat eggs and milk until frothy. Pour just enough of the egg mixture into the baking dish to cover the bottom. Arrange the sandwiches on top. Pour the remaining egg mixture over the top. Bake for 20 minutes, or until golden and set.

OPTIONAL: Yummy drizzled with pure maple syrup.

Basic Crepes

MAKES 35

*Serve with Toffee Bananas (page 37) or,
as the French do, with Nutella.*

3 eggs

1½ cups milk

2¼ cups GF all-purpose flour

1 tablespoon olive oil

In a bowl, with an electric mixer, beat together the eggs, milk, flour, and 1½ cups water. Heat a nonstick 8-inch skillet and add the oil, swirling it around to coat the entire surface. Poor in enough batter to coat the bottom of the pan, swirling in a circular motion so the batter is even. Cook until the bottom is light brown, about 2 minutes, then flip over to cook the other side.

NOTE: This batter will keep for a couple of days in the refrigerator.

Bircher Muesli

SERVES 1

Don't peel the apple: the skin is rich in nutrients.

½ cup GF muesli

¼ cup orange juice

2 tablespoons plain yogurt

1 Granny Smith apple, grated

Soak the muesli in the juice for 15 minutes. Mix in the remaining ingredients.

Breakfast Berry Parfait

SERVES 1

8 ounces GF yogurt

1½ teaspoons honey

½ cup sliced strawberries

¼ cup blueberries

Combine the yogurt and honey. Spoon one-third of the yogurt into a large glass, then add a layer of fruit. Repeat twice, ending with a fruit layer.

OPTIONAL: Garnish by sprinkling with a little shredded mint.

Buckwheat Pancakes

SERVES 2

Recipe by Melissa Perran.

1 cup buckwheat flour

1 egg

2 tablespoons butter, melted

2 tablespoons pure maple syrup

In a bowl, mix all the ingredients together with 1 cup water. Add a bit more water if the batter seems too thick. Heat a nonstick skillet over medium heat. Dollop in the batter and cook the pancakes for 1 minute. Flip them over and cook for another minute.

OPTIONAL: Top with fresh fruit, jam, or cream. Substitute GF self-rising flour for the buckwheat flour.

Cheese Omelet

SERVES 2

3 eggs, separated

½ cup grated cheese

1 tablespoon butter

In a bowl, beat the egg whites until stiff. Lightly fold the egg whites into the beaten yolks. Add 3 tablespoons cold water, the cheese, and a pinch of sea salt. In a nonstick skillet, melt the butter. Pour in the egg mixture and cook until golden underneath. Flip with a spatula.

NOTE: Water gives the omelet a fluffy texture.

Citrus Pancakes

SERVES 4

2 tangerines

1 cup GF self-rising flour

1 egg

1 cup milk

Grate the zest from the tangerines, then separate into segments and chop. In a bowl, combine the flour, egg, and a pinch of sea salt. Gradually beat in the milk until the batter is thick and smooth. Add the tangerine zest and segments. Heat a nonstick skillet. Pour the batter in to make whatever size pancakes you want. Cook until bubbling on top, then flip and cook the second side.

OPTIONAL: Serve with pure maple syrup, lemon juice and sugar, honey, or stewed fruits. Another tasty topping is citrus-infused maple syrup: add strips of orange peel to a bowl of pure maple syrup and let sit for 1 hour before using.

Date Loaf
SERVES 6 TO 8

A recipe from Mrs. Frasier, Raceview, Queensland.
Absolutely divine! Serve warm with lots of butter.

2 teaspoons instant coffee

12 ounces dates, chopped

1 generous cup GF self-
   rising flour

¼ cup sliced almonds

Dissolve the coffee in 1 cup boiling water. Pour over the dates and let soak overnight. Preheat the oven to 325°F. Line a 9 by 5 by 3-inch loaf pan with parchment paper. Stir the flour into the date mixture to make a batter and scrape the batter into the loaf pan. Sprinkle with the almonds and bake for 45 minutes.

Feta & Leek Omelet
SERVES 2

1 tablespoon butter

1 leek, thinly sliced

4 eggs, beaten

4 ounces feta cheese,
   crumbled

In a nonstick skillet, heat the butter. Add the leek and stir-fry for 3 to 4 minutes, or until soft, taking care not to burn. Pour in the eggs, season with sea salt and pepper, and cook over medium heat for 5 minutes, or until the eggs are no longer runny. Sprinkle with the feta, fold in half, and let sit for the feta to warm through. Cut into wedges to serve.

Ham & Egg Quiche

MAKES 6

From Sharyn Seligmann . . . Faaabalish!

6 round slices GF ham

6 eggs

1 cup grated Monterey Jack cheese

2 tablespoons chopped fresh parsley

Preheat the oven to 350°F. Line 6 large nonstick muffin cups with the ham. Beat the eggs with sea salt and pepper to taste. Pour the eggs into the ham-lined muffin cups. Top with the Montery Jack and parsley. Bake for 20 minutes, or until set.

OPTIONAL: Instead of parsley, these could be topped with tomato or bell pepper.

Quick Muffins

MAKES 6

1¾ cups GF self-rising flour

¼ cup GF mayonnaise

1 cup milk

4 slices bacon, diced and fried

Preheat the oven to 350°F. Mix all the ingredients until just combined. Fill 6 muffin cups two-thirds full. Bake for 20 to 25 minutes.

OPTIONAL: Swap out the bacon for whatever you like—ham, chives, sun-dried tomatoes, feta cheese—as long as it is gluten-free.

Raspberry Delights

SERVES 4

1 pint raspberries

1⅔ cups plain Greek yogurt

1 tablespoon finely grated lemon zest

In a blender, puree the raspberries until just smooth. In a small bowl, combine the yogurt and lemon zest. Gently swirl the raspberry puree into the yogurt mixture. Spoon into 4 dessert glasses and refrigerate for 15 minutes before serving.

OPTIONAL: Drizzle with honey to serve.

Scones

MAKES 12

4 cups GF self-rising flour

1¼ cups light cream

1 cup Sprite

Preheat the oven to 400°F. Line a baking sheet with parchment paper. Sift the self-rising flour into a bowl. Make a well in the center and pour in the cream and ¾ cup of the Sprite. Mix to make a firm dough (if too wet, add more flour; if too dry, add more Sprite). Turn out onto a floured surface and knead into a 3-inch-high round mound. Cut with a 3-inch scone cutter and place the scones on the baking sheet close together. Bake for 15 minutes, or until golden brown.

OPTIONAL: For savory scones, substitute seltzer for the Sprite and add sun-dried tomatoes or Parmesan cheese or your favorite herbs.

Sweet Breakfast Toast

MAKES 1

Recipe by Cyndi O'Meara.

1 slice GF bread

1 teaspoon peanut butter

1 teaspoon honey

1 small banana, mashed

Toast the bread. Spread it with the peanut butter, honey, and banana in layers.

OPTIONAL: Sprinkle with pine nuts.

Toffee Bananas

SERVES 4

Serve wrapped in GF crepes . . . Yummmmmmmmmmm!

3 tablespoons butter

½ cup packed light brown sugar

3 or 4 bananas, sliced

In a nonstick skillet, heat the butter over medium heat. Add the brown sugar and stir until dissolved. Add the banana slices and cook until warmed through.

Tru-Blu Eggs

MAKES 4

12 asparagus spears

4 eggs

4 ounces blue Brie cheese, sliced, at room temperature

¼ cup garlic oil (see Note)

Bring a skillet of salted water to a boil. Add the asparagus and cook for 2 minutes, or until tender. Remove and set aside. Fill a large saucepan three-fourths full with water and bring to a boil. Stir the water clockwise rapidly, and gently crack the eggs into the swirling water one after the other (the moving water helps the eggs roll and form separate balls). Reduce to a light simmer. Poach for 1 to 2 minutes for medium yolks, 3 minutes for firm yolks. With a slotted spoon, carefully lift the eggs from the water, letting them drain. Place 3 asparagus spears on a plate, put an egg on top of the asparagus, and put the blue Brie on top of the egg. Drizzle with garlic oil.

NOTE: To make your own garlic oil, fill a sealable jar with 1 cup extra virgin olive oil. Add 3 split cloves of garlic. Let sit overnight for the flavor to infuse before using.

APPETIZERS

From small beginnings come great things.

—Proverb

Asparagus Wraps

SERVES 6

2 bunches asparagus

8 slices prosciutto, cut lengthwise into ½-inch-wide strips

2 tablespoons extra virgin olive oil

2 tablespoons balsamic vinegar

Preheat the oven to 350°F. Wrap a strip of prosciutto around each asparagus spear, creating a long, spiral effect. Place the spears on a baking sheet, drizzle with the oil, and season with sea salt and pepper to taste. Bake for 5 to 6 minutes. Transfer carefully to a plate and serve trickled with the balsamic vinegar.

Baked Camembert with Caramelized Macadamias

SERVES 4

Try this! Serve with your favorite GF crackers.

1 small wheel (about 4 ounces) Camembert cheese

1 cup sugar

1 cup roasted macadamia nuts, chopped

Place the Camembert wheel on a heatproof plate or platter. In a heavy-bottomed saucepan, cook the sugar over low heat, without stirring, for 1 to 2 minutes, or until melted and dark golden brown. You may need to tilt the pan to ensure that the sugar melts evenly. Add the nuts and stir to coat. Remove from the heat and set aside until the bubbles subside. Pour the caramelized nuts over the cheese. The caramel will soften and seep into the cheese, giving it a bittersweet flavor. Serve immediately.

Bite-Size Fried Haloumi

SERVES 4

2 tablespoons GF all-purpose flour

8 ounces haloumi cheese, drained and cut into 1-inch cubes

3 tablespoons olive oil

2 tablespoons fresh lemon juice

Place the flour on a plate and season with sea salt and pepper. Add the haloumi and evenly coat. In a nonstick skillet, heat the oil over high heat. Add the haloumi and cook, turning occasionally, for 2 minutes, or until golden brown. Transfer to a serving plate, sprinkle with the lemon juice, and season with pepper to taste.

Chicken & Chorizo Skewers

SERVES 4

1 pound skinless, boneless chicken breasts, cut into 1-inch pieces

1 pound chorizo sausage, sliced into rounds

1 large red bell pepper, cut into 1-inch pieces

2 tablespoons olive oil

Thread the chicken, chorizo, and pepper onto skewers, alternating the ingredients. Season with sea salt and pepper and brush with the olive oil. Grill for 12 to 15 minutes, or until the chicken is cooked through.

SERVING SUGGESTION: These are delicious served warm with a yummy salsa or Cumin Aioli (page 10) for dipping.

Date & Walnut Pears

SERVES 4

1 large ripe pear

1 tablespoon cream cheese

2 dates, pitted and finely chopped

1½ tablespoons finely chopped walnuts

Quarter the pear lengthwise and remove the core. In a small bowl, combine the remaining ingredients. Serve the pear quarters with a dollop of the date-walnut cream.

Deviled Eggs

SERVES 6

A recipe from Marie McColl.

6 hard-boiled eggs, peeled and halved lengthwise

2 teaspoons chopped parsley, plus more for garnish

1 to 2 tablespoons GF Dijon mustard

Spoon the yolks out of the eggs into a bowl and mash with a fork. Stir in the 2 teaspoons parsley and enough mustard to give a soft consistency. Spoon the mixture back into the egg whites and refrigerate. Serve garnished with parsley and seasoned with sea salt and pepper.

OPTIONAL: Use 1 tablespoon Dijon mustard and 1 tablespoon GF mayo for a milder flavor.

Dipping Chips

SERVES 4 TO 6

These are divine!

4 GF tortillas (10-inch)

2 tablespoons olive oil

1 tablespoon fresh rosemary leaves, finely chopped

Preheat the oven to 350°F. Brush the tortillas with the oil and sprinkle with the rosemary and 1 teaspoon sea salt. Cut into wedges. Place on a baking sheet and bake for 5 to 7 minutes, or until browned on the edges and crisp. Serve with dips.

Fried Calamari

SERVES 4 TO 6

These are quick, easy, and ALWAYS a hit!

3 cups GF all-purpose flour

4 tablespoons herb seasoning

4 cleaned squid, cut into ¾-inch-wide rings or strips

2 cups sunflower oil

In a bowl, combine the flour with the herb seasoning and add the squid. Toss until the squid is coated with the mixture, then gently shake off the excess flour. In a medium saucepan, heat the oil until sizzling. Working in batches, add a few pieces of squid at a time (take care not to add too many so they don't stick together) and cook for 1 to 2 minutes. With a slotted spoon, transfer the squid to paper towels to drain. Serve warm.

OPTIONAL: Delicious served with Lemon Aioli (page 15) or Cumin Aioli (page 10).

Fried Chorizo with Garlic

SERVES 6

4 GF cured chorizo sausages, sliced

2 cloves garlic, finely chopped

4 sprigs flat-leaf parsley, chopped

In a large skillet, cook the sausage slices, stirring, until crisp. Drain off the excess fat. Return the sausage slices to the pan, add the garlic, and heat through. Just before serving, toss with the parsley.

Garlic Crisps

SERVES 4

These are a lighter option for use as a side dish or as dippers.

2 tablespoons butter, at room temperature

2 tablespoons garlic, crushed through a press

2 GF tortillas (10-inch)

Preheat the oven to 350°F. Line a baking sheet with parchment paper. In a small bowl, blend together the butter and garlic. Spread liberally over each tortilla. Cut the tortillas into wedges and place on the baking sheet. Bake for 10 minutes, or until lightly crispy.

Marinated & Baked Olives

SERVES 6

1 pound pitted mixed olives

Grated zest from 1 lemon

2 sprigs rosemary, leaves only, chopped

2 cloves garlic, thinly sliced

Preheat the oven to 375°F. Place the olives in a baking dish and, with a rolling pin, gently push down so the skin splits further. Mix in the lemon zest, rosemary, and garlic. Bake for 15 minutes and serve while warm.

OPTIONAL: Add 1 tablespoon olive oil to the mix.

Minted Lamb Balls

SERVES 4

A recipe from Janelle McCosker.

1 pound ground lamb

2 teaspoons GF curry powder

6 to 8 sprigs mint, chopped

In a large bowl, combine all the ingredients. Roll into bite-size balls. In a large nonstick skillet, cook the meatballs until crunchy on the outside (this means they are cooked well on the inside).

OPTIONAL: These are lovely served with Raita (page 20) or Cumin Aioli (page 10) as a dipping sauce.

Parmesan Crisps

MAKES 6

A recipe by Lorraine Leeson . . . D.I.V.I.N.E!!!! Serve as a nibble with drinks or as an accompaniment to your meal.

8-ounce piece of Parmesan cheese

1 tablespoon sesame seeds

Preheat the oven to 400°F. Line a baking sheet with parchment paper. Space 6 egg rings evenly on the sheet. Into each, finely grate enough Parmesan to completely cover the paper. Top with a sprinkle of sesame seeds and gently remove the egg rings. Bake for 5 to 6 minutes, or until the cheese melts into lacy disks. Let cool before serving.

OPTIONAL: Instead of sesame seeds, use a sprinkle of smoked paprika or a smattering of your favorite fresh herb.

Pear & Roquefort Bites

MAKES 16

2 ripe pears, peeled

4 ounces Roquefort cheese

Cut the pears and Roquefort into small cubes. Thread one cube of each onto a toothpick and serve immediately.

Ricotta & Prosciutto Baked Pies

MAKES 12

A recipe from the vibrant Perditta O'Connor.

6 slices prosciutto, halved

1 container (15 ounces) ricotta cheese

Fresh thyme leaves from 6 sprigs

6 chives, chopped

Preheat the oven to 350°F. Line the bottom and sides of 6 mini muffin cups with the prosciutto. In a bowl, combine the ricotta, thyme, and chives. Season with sea salt and pepper. Divide the mixture evenly among the muffin cups. Bake for 15 minutes, or until set. Set aside to cool for 15 minutes before serving.

OPTIONAL: Bake topped with some halved cherry tomatoes.

Salmon Pâté

MAKES 1 CUP

Serve with your favorite GF crackers.

1 can (7 ounces) pink salmon, drained and bones removed

4 tablespoons cream cheese, at room temperature

1 tablespoon GF mayonnaise

1 tablespoon fresh lemon juice

In a food processor, combine all the ingredients and blend until smooth. Season with sea salt and pepper to taste and blend again.

Spinach & Cashew Pâté

MAKES 1 CUP

8 ounces fresh spinach leaves

4 ounces cashews

½ teaspoon grated nutmeg

In a vegetable steamer, steam the spinach until just wilted. In a blender, blitz the cashews until finely ground. Add the spinach and nutmeg. Blend to combine.

OPTIONAL: Add 1 generous tablespoon blue cheese.

Strawberry Sweet & Sour

SERVES 4

A recipe from Lorraine Leeson.

¼ cup packed light brown sugar

½ cup sour cream

1 pint strawberries

Place the brown sugar and sour cream in separate serving bowls. Serve the strawberries for dipping first into the sour cream and then into the sugar. . . . Savor the flavor!

OPTIONAL: Rach and Kim have a fourth ingredient with this one—a glass of bubbles—enjoy!

NOTE: Always wash strawberries before you remove their stems; otherwise water will get into the fruit and spoil their flavor.

Tangy Cheese Balls

MAKES 24

4 ounces cream cheese, at room temperature

2 tablespoons finely crumbled blue cheese

2 tablespoons grated orange zest

2 ounces mixed nuts, finely chopped

In a small bowl, combine the cream cheese, blue cheese, and orange zest. Form into small balls and roll in the nuts. Chill for 1 hour, or until firm, before serving.

Teriyaki Scallops

SERVES 4

A recipe from the talented Dan Primmer, chef extraordinaire!

16 scallops

½ cup GF teriyaki sauce

2 tablespoons diced pickled ginger

1 tablespoon toasted sesame seeds

Marinate the scallops in the teriyaki sauce for 1 hour. Pour into a skillet and cook over medium heat for 5 minutes, flipping the scallops halfway through. Serve as an appetizer on Chinese soupspoons, garnished with the ginger and sprinkled with the sesame seeds.

Wheel of Brie

SERVES 4

This is sensational served with your favorite GF crackers.

4-ounce wheel of Brie cheese

1 tablespoon GF basil pesto

1 ounce marinated roasted red peppers, sliced

2 tablespoons pine nuts

Preheat the oven to 300°F. Line a baking sheet with parchment paper. Place the Brie on the baking sheet and gently cut the top rind off the wheel and discard. Smear the cheese with the pesto, top with the peppers, and sprinkle with the pine nuts. Bake for 5 to 10 minutes, or until it becomes soft and gooey.

LIGHT LUNCHES

*If every day is an awakening, you will never grow old.
You will just keep growing.*

—Gail Sheehy

Asparagus Soup

SERVES 4

4 cups GF chicken or vegetable stock

2 bunches asparagus, cut into ¾- to 1-inch pieces

½ cup heavy cream

Cayenne pepper

In a large nonstick saucepan, bring the stock and asparagus to a simmer. Cook for 5 minutes, or until the asparagus is tender but still green. Remove from the heat and puree using a handheld blender. Return to low heat, add the cream, and cook on low until heated through. Season with sea salt and cayenne pepper to taste. Serve hot.

NOTE: Fresh asparagus will snap when it's bent. And where it snaps naturally indicates the boundary between the edible part and the tough, inedible end, which is fibrous and stringy.

Bacon & Egg Quiches
MAKES 12

Recipe by AJ Gregory.

5 slices bacon, thinly sliced

5 eggs

1 cup light cream

6 button mushrooms, sliced

Preheat the oven to 375°F. In a nonstick skillet, cook the bacon until lightly golden brown. Drain on paper towels. In a bowl, beat the eggs and cream together. Stir in the mushrooms and bacon. Divide the mixture among 12 cups of a nonstick muffin tin. Bake for 7 to 8 minutes, or until a light golden brown. Turn out and serve.

OPTIONAL: Stir one of these fillings into the egg mixture: finely chopped leek (high in antioxidants), finely chopped scallions, chopped parsley, pine nuts, feta cheese. Or top with a small roasted cherry tomato.

Baked Peppers
SERVES 2

Delicious served with a fresh green salad.

2 red bell peppers, halved lengthwise

2 cups leftover Bolognese sauce

⅓ cup grated Parmesan cheese

Preheat the oven to 350°F. Line a baking sheet with parchment paper. Place the peppers on the baking sheet and fill with Bolognese sauce. Top with the Parmesan and bake for 20 minutes.

NOTE: The difference between red, yellow, and green peppers is that red are ripe, yellow are nearly ripe, and green aren't!

Baked Potato with Tomato Salsa

SERVES 1

1 large (8-ounce) baking potato

¼ cup low-fat cottage cheese

2 tablespoons salsa

1 tablespoon chopped fresh chives

Preheat the oven to 350°F. Pierce the potato several times with a knife. Wrap the potato in foil and bake for 30 to 40 minutes, or until fork-tender. Let stand for 5 minutes, then remove the foil and cut a crisscross halfway into the potato. Gently squeeze the potato to form an opening. Add the cottage cheese. Top with the salsa and sprinkle with the chives.

OPTIONAL: Add one of these fillings to the potato: GF taco sauce, sour cream, and mashed avocado; tuna; GF coleslaw and grated cheese; chili con carne, sour cream, and chives; GF baked beans and grated cheese; GF korma sauce, sour cream, and cilantro.

Beef Koftas

MAKES 4 TO 6

½ cup crunchy peanut butter

2 teaspoons GF curry powder

1 egg

1 pound lean ground beef

In a microwaveable bowl, warm the peanut butter on high for 30 seconds to soften. Stir in the curry powder and egg. In a large bowl, blend the ground beef with the peanut butter mixture. Roll the mixture into fat sausage shapes using ½ cup of mixture for each kofta. Cook under the broiler or on the grill until cooked through.

OPTIONAL: Serve as a burger or on GF bread with Satay Sauce (page 23) and salad or separately as a patty with vegetables . . . Mmmmm!

Butternut Squash, Lentil & Ginger Soup

SERVES 4

½ cup red lentils, rinsed

2¼ pounds butternut squash, peeled and cut into chunks

1 tablespoon grated fresh ginger

4 cups GF vegetable stock

In a large saucepan, combine all the ingredients plus sea salt and pepper to taste. Cook over medium heat for 30 minutes. Transfer to a blender and puree.

Carrot & Cilantro Soup

SERVES 8

8 cups GF vegetable stock

1 large onion, chopped

6 sprigs cilantro, with roots, coarsely chopped

8 carrots, coarsely chopped

In a saucepan, combine the stock, onion, cilantro, and carrots. Bring to a boil. Reduce to a simmer and cook until the carrots are tender. Season with pepper to taste. Transfer to a blender and puree.

OPTIONAL: Before serving, swirl in some sour cream.

Cheese & Garlic Pizza

SERVES 2

A recipe from Anthony "Spud" Moore.

16 cloves garlic

3 GF tortillas (10-inch)

4 ounces Parmesan cheese, grated

4 ounces mozzarella cheese, shredded

Preheat the oven to 450°F. Peel the garlic, wrap in foil, and roast for 15 minutes. Let cool. (Leave the oven on.) Spread 1 tortilla with one-third of the garlic, Parmesan, and mozzarella. Repeat the layering two more times, using all the ingredients. Place on a baking sheet and bake for 15 minutes, or until the cheeses bubble and turn golden brown. Let cool slightly and cut into wedges.

Chicken Salad

SERVES 4

A recipe from Lisa Darr.

1 boneless, skinless chicken breast, grilled and sliced

½ cup green grapes, halved

2 or 3 celery stalks, thinly sliced

2 tablespoons orange juice

In a large bowl, combine the chicken, grapes, and celery and toss well. Drizzle the orange juice over the salad and season with sea salt and pepper to taste.

Chorizo & Pepper Soup

SERVES 4 TO 6

This is REALLLLLLLY TASTY!

2 GF cured chorizo sausages, diced

4 red bell peppers, diced

1 can (14.5 ounces) whole peeled tomatoes

3 cups GF chicken stock

In a nonstick skillet, cook the chorizos for 5 minutes. Drain on paper towels. In the same skillet with the chorizo juices, cook the peppers for 5 minutes, then stir in the tomatoes. Season with sea salt and pepper to taste. Add the stock and bring to a boil. Reduce to a simmer and cook until the peppers are tender. Transfer the soup to a blender and puree. Serve garnished with the chorizo.

Corn & Chicken Soup

SERVES 4

Recipe from Michelle Ashdown. Serve with GF toast.

4 cups GF chicken stock

1 pound boneless, skinless chicken breasts, thinly sliced

2 cans (14.7 ounces each) GF creamed corn

4 eggs, lightly beaten

In a large nonstick saucepan, bring the stock to a boil. Add the chicken, reduce to a simmer, and cook for 3 minutes. Add the creamed corn and simmer for 8 minutes. Whisk in the eggs and cook, whisking, until the egg forms strands that are spread evenly throughout the soup. Season with sea salt and pepper to taste. Serve hot.

Curried Butternut Squash Soup

SERVES 4

2¼ pounds butternut squash, peeled and chopped

1 generous teaspoon GF curry powder

1 clove garlic, crushed through a press

⅔ cup heavy cream

In a saucepan, combine the squash, curry powder, garlic, and 2 cups water. Bring to a boil. Reduce to a simmer and cook for 20 minutes, or until the squash is tender. Transfer to a blender and puree. Stir in the cream.

Easy Eggplant Grill

SERVES 2

This is a glorious lunch served with a fresh green salad.

12 ounces eggplant, cut crosswise into 8 thick slices

2 teaspoons olive oil

1 cup GF marinara sauce, heated

¼ cup shredded Cheddar cheese

Preheat the broiler. Line a baking sheet with foil. Brush the eggplant slices with the oil and place on the baking sheet. Season with sea salt and pepper to taste. Broil for 3 minutes, or until golden. Turn and broil for 3 minutes on the second side. Spoon 2 tablespoons of the marinara sauce onto each slice and sprinkle with Cheddar. Broil for 3 minutes, or until the cheese is golden.

Gourmet Pizza

MAKES 4

4 GF tortillas (8-inch)

4 generous teaspoons GF basil pesto

16 slices GF salami or paper-thin GF ham, torn

1½ cups shredded mozzarella cheese

Preheat the broiler. Broil the tortillas for 1 minute to toast. Remove (but leave the broiler on) and spread the untoasted side with pesto. Top with the ham and sprinkle with the mozzarella. Season with pepper to taste. Return to the broiler for 3 to 4 minutes, or until the cheese has melted and turned golden brown.

Kabocha Squash Soup

SERVES 4

This is so easy. Serve with hot GF toast or GF croutons.

1 kabocha squash, peeled and cut into chunks

1¾ cups evaporated milk

3 tablespoons chopped parsley

In a saucepan of boiling water, cook the squash until tender. Drain and transfer to a bowl. Mash well, gradually adding the evaporated milk until the mixture is a soupy consistency. Season with sea salt and pepper to taste. Garnish with the parsley.

OPTIONAL: Stir in ¼ cup crunchy peanut butter and a handful of chopped cilantro.

Pea & Ham Soup

SERVES 4 TO 6

This is really tasty! Serve with your favorite GF bread.

2¼ pounds smoked ham hocks

8 ounces dried whole peas

2 onions, coarsely chopped

In a large saucepan, combine all the ingredients and add 10 cups water. Bring to a boil, then reduce to a simmer and cook for 1 hour. Remove from the heat and let cool. Remove the meat from the hocks and return to the pot. Transfer to a blender and puree. Add water if the soup is too thick.

Quesadillas

SERVES 4

1 tablespoon butter

8 GF corn tortillas (8-inch)

2 vine-ripened tomatoes, sliced

4 ounces Cheddar cheese, shredded

In a nonstick skillet, melt the butter over medium heat. Lay 4 tortillas on a work surface and top with the tomatoes and Cheddar. Season with sea salt and pepper to taste. Top with the remaining tortillas. Working in batches, add the quesadillas to the skillet and cook over medium heat for 2 minutes, or until the bottom tortilla is crisp and golden. Flip and repeat. Cut into wedges to serve.

OPTIONAL: Add some GF mango chutney, tomato relish, or mustard of choice to the tomatoes and Cheddar. Or try one of these fillings: refried beans, red chili sauce, and grated cheese; cheese and fresh basil; avocado, cooked chicken, and mozzarella.

Salmon & Camembert Omelet

SERVES 4

A recipe from the very generous Marie McColl.

8 eggs

1 teaspoon butter

5 ounces smoked salmon

4-ounce wheel Camembert cheese, sliced

In a bowl, beat the eggs with ⅓ cup water. Season with sea salt and pepper. Lightly grease a small nonstick skillet with a little of the butter. Add ½ cup of the egg mixture, tilting the pan for even coverage. Cook for 2 minutes, or until just set. Place one-fourth of the salmon and Camembert over half the omelet, fold the omelet over, and cook until the cheese just starts to melt. Repeat the process three more times.

OPTIONAL: Replace the smoked salmon with a can of pink salmon, drained and flaked, and substitute shredded Cheddar cheese for the Camembert.

Salmon & Caper Salad

SERVES 4

1 can (5 ounces) salmon, drained

4 ounces feta cheese, crumbled

4 ounces baby arugula

1 tablespoon drained capers, chopped

Simply mix and enjoy!

Salt & Pepper Calamari

SERVES 6

Y.u.m.m.y!

1 teaspoon Szechuan peppercorns

1 cup cornstarch

14 ounces cleaned squid

1 cup sunflower oil

In a dry skillet, roast the peppercorns until they are fragrant and begin to crackle. Transfer to a mortar along with 1 teaspoon sea salt and grind. In a shallow bowl, combine the cornstarch and salt and pepper mixture. Dredge the squid in the mixture, shaking off any excess. In a wok, heat the oil until very hot. Working in batches, cook the squid for 1 minute, or until cooked. Drain on paper towels and serve hot.

Shrimp & Mango Salad

SERVES 4

Quick, easy, and delicious!

12 large peeled and deveined cooked jumbo shrimp

1 cucumber, thinly sliced lengthwise

4 ounces unsalted roasted cashews

1 large mango

In a bowl, combine the shrimp, cucumber, and cashews. Cut the mango off the pit, slice the flesh, and add to the salad. Squeeze the flesh remaining around the pit to get the juice and add to the salad. Lightly toss the salad and serve.

Spicy Chorizo Wedges

SERVES 2

1 GF cured chorizo sausage, chopped into small pieces

3 eggs, beaten

2 GF tortillas (8-inch)

½ bunch watercress

In a medium nonstick skillet, cook the chorizo for 2 to 3 minutes, or until browned. Set the chorizo aside, leaving the juices in the skillet. Season the eggs with sea salt and pepper to taste. Add the eggs to the skillet and cook until bubbles appear. Add the chorizo and flip after 1 minute. When set, lay the omelet on a tortilla. Scatter with cress. Top with the second tortilla and cut into wedges.

Summer Rolls

SERVES 4

14 ounces ground pork

⅓ cup GF oyster sauce

8 Thai spring roll wrappers

2 ounces snow peas, sliced

In a nonstick skillet, brown the pork, breaking it up with a spoon. Season with sea salt and pepper to taste. Stir in the oyster sauce. Remove from the heat and let cool. Working with one at a time, soak a spring roll wrapper in water for 20 seconds (no longer, or it will fall apart). Remove and place on a work surface. Spread one-fourth of the pork mixture across the bottom half of each wrapper and top with one-fourth of the snow peas. Fold the bottom up, then fold the sides in. Roll up burrito style. Cut in half and serve immediately.

OPTIONAL: Serve with some GF Thai sweet chili sauce for dipping.

NOTE: Don't be tempted to overfill as we first did, because the wrapper will split.

Sweet Chili & Chicken Salad

SERVES 2 TO 4

A recipe from Glen Turnbull.

2 cups shredded cooked chicken

½ head iceberg lettuce, shredded

2 tablespoons GF Thai sweet chili sauce

1 tablespoon GF sour cream

In a bowl, toss the chicken and lettuce together. Mix the sweet chili sauce and sour cream together, add to the bowl, and toss to combine well.

OPTIONAL: Add some thinly sliced Spanish onion and sprinkle with crushed GF corn chips.

Tandoori Wings

SERVES 4 TO 6

D.e.l.i.c.i.o.u.s.

⅓ cup GF tandoori paste

⅓ cup plain yogurt

1 yellow onion, grated

2¼ pounds chicken wings

In a large bowl, combine the tandoori paste, yogurt, and onion. Add the wings and coat generously. Cover and refrigerate for at least 3 hours. Preheat the oven to 400°F. Place the wings on an oiled wire rack set inside a larger shallow baking pan. Roast, uncovered, for 30 minutes, or until the chicken is well browned and cooked through.

Thai Butternut Squash Soup

SERVES 4

A recipe from Anthony "Spud" Moore. THAI-RRIFIC!!

2¼ pounds butternut squash, diced

2 tablespoons GF red curry paste

1¼ cups coconut cream

8 sprigs cilantro, chopped

In a large skillet, cook the butternut squash and red curry paste until the mixture starts to catch on the saucepan. Add the coconut cream to deglaze the pan, then top with enough water to be level with the squash. Bring to a boil. Reduce to a simmer and cook until the squash is very soft. Transfer to a blender and puree. Stir in the cilantro.

Toasted Camembert Sandwich

MAKES 2

Yummy!

1 tablespoon butter

4 slices GF bread

3 ounces Camembert cheese, thickly sliced

2 tablespoons cranberry sauce

Butter one side of each slice of bread. Lay the Camembert on the unbuttered side of 2 of the slices. Dollop the cheese with a spoonful of cranberry sauce. Top with the remaining slices of bread, butter side up. Cook in a nonstick skillet for a couple of minutes on each side, pressing down with a metal spatula to flatten. When the cheese is warm and melting, remove, cut, and serve hot immediately.

OPTIONAL: Drizzle the Camembert and cranberry with a little balsamic vinegar before toasting.

Tomato & Basil Soup

SERVES 4

A recipe from Marie McColl.

3 cans (14.5 ounces each) whole tomatoes

2 cups GF vegetable stock

Basil leaves from ½ bunch

2 tablespoons light brown sugar

In a saucepan, combine all the ingredients, plus pepper to taste. Gently bring to a boil. Transfer to a blender and puree.

NOTE: If any of your hot soups end up slightly salty, add a whole peeled potato and simmer for about 15 minutes to absorb the salt. Remove the potato and serve on the side.

Tomato Soup

SERVES 4

A recipe from the lovely Michelle Dodd, who says, "This is a deliciously rich-flavored soup!"

10 plum tomatoes, halved lengthwise

¼ cup olive oil

Thyme leaves from 4 sprigs

2 cups GF vegetable stock

Preheat the oven to 300°F. Place the tomatoes on a baking sheet and, using a pastry brush, brush with the olive oil. Sprinkle with the thyme and season with sea salt and pepper to taste. Bake for 30 to 45 minutes. In a food processor or blender, puree the tomatoes with the vegetable stock. Heat through in a saucepan and serve hot.

Tostadas

SERVES 4

4 GF tortillas (8-inch)

½ cup chunky tomato salsa

1 can (15 ounces) Mexican-style refried beans

4 ounces Cheddar cheese, shredded

Preheat the oven to 400°F. Line 2 baking sheets with parchment paper. Place the tortillas on the baking sheets and spread with the salsa. In a bowl, combine the beans and Cheddar. Spoon the mixture evenly on top of the tortillas. Bake for 10 minutes, or until the tortillas are golden and crisp.

OPTIONAL: Top with Guacamole (page 14).

Vegetable Croutons

SERVES 4

A recipe by Lorraine Leeson. Serve as a garnish for soup. AJ Gregory says these are also fantastic sprinkled over a salad.

¼ cup olive oil

1 small sweet potato or parsnip, peeled and cubed

1 clove garlic

In a large pan, heat the oil. Add the vegetable cubes and garlic and cook for 10 minutes, or until tender and lightly browned. Drain on paper towels and sprinkle over the soup or salad.

Vegetable Gazpacho

SERVES 4

7 plum tomatoes, halved

½ hothouse (seedless) cucumber, chopped

½ bunch cilantro, with some sprigs reserved for garnish

½ cup red wine vinegar

In a food processor, combine all the ingredients and blend for 1 minute. Season with sea salt and pepper to taste. To serve, pour into 4 martini glasses and garnish with cilantro sprigs.

Zucchini Slice

SERVES 8

3 zucchini, grated

4 slices bacon, finely diced

1 cup GF self-rising flour

6 eggs, beaten

Preheat the oven to 350°F. Line an 11 by 7-inch baking dish with parchment paper. In a bowl, combine all the ingredients. Season well with sea salt and pepper. Pour the mixture into the baking dish and bake for 25 to 30 minutes. Serve hot, sliced into long fingers.

OPTIONAL: Add a dash of paprika to the mixture and sprinkle with grated Cheddar cheese before baking.

SIDES

One cannot think well, love well, sleep well,
if one has not dined well.

—Virginia Woolf

SALADS

Arugula & Parmesan Salad

SERVES 4

A recipe from the clever Cheyne McCorkindale.

4 ounces baby arugula

1 tablespoon extra virgin olive oil

½ Spanish onion, finely sliced

2 ounces Parmesan cheese, finely grated

In a serving bowl, combine the arugula and oil. Add the onion and Parmesan and toss to coat well.

Asparagus with Macadamia & Cranberry Dressing

SERVES 4

2 bunches asparagus

2 ounces roasted macadamia nuts, finely chopped

⅓ cup dried cranberries, finely chopped

¼ cup red wine vinegar

In a large saucepan of boiling water, cook the asparagus for 2 to 3 minutes, or until bright green. Drain and rinse under cold water. Lay out on a platter. Meanwhile, in a nonstick skillet, toss the macadamias and cranberries until warmed. Add the vinegar and stir to combine. Gently spoon the mixture over the asparagus.

Basil & Lentil Salad

SERVES 6

This is faaaaaaaaaaaaabulous!

2 bunches basil

1 can (15 ounces) brown lentils, drained

8 ounces cherry tomatoes, halved

½ Spanish onion, thinly sliced

Tear the basil leaves from the stems and place the leaves in a salad bowl. Add the remaining ingredients and toss to combine.

OPTIONAL: Serve drizzled with Classic Salad Dressing (page 8).

NOTE: Basil leaves are best torn or used whole rather than cut with a knife, as they bruise easily. The herb is best used raw, as cooking diminishes its flavor.

Caprese Salad

SERVES 4

This is a tasty southern Italian salad named for the island of Capri.

6 vine-ripened tomatoes, thickly sliced

2 tablespoons extra virgin olive oil

4 ounces fresh buffalo mozzarella, thickly sliced

16 fresh basil leaves

Arrange the tomatoes on a large flat serving plate; don't worry if they overlap. Drizzle with the oil and top with the mozzarella and basil. Season generously with sea salt and pepper. Cover and chill before serving.

NOTE: This salad is best eaten while listening to a Frank Sinatra CD and drinking a glass of wine!

Carrot, Raisin & Celery Salad

SERVES 6

4 carrots, grated

1 cup raisins

2 celery stalks, thinly sliced

¼ cup GF mayonnaise

Mix all the ingredients together and chill before serving.

OPTIONAL: Substitute fresh pineapple for the celery.

Cherry Tomato & Cucumber Salad

SERVES 6

4 ounces mixed greens

4 ounces cherry tomatoes, halved

1 cucumber, thinly sliced

¼ cup balsamic and roasted garlic salad dressing

In a salad bowl, combine the greens, tomatoes, and cucumber. Drizzle with the dressing and toss gently to combine.

OPTIONAL: Any balsamic-based salad dressing is nice.

Feta & Watermelon Salad

SERVES 6

2½ pounds watermelon, seeded and cubed

2 tablespoons finely chopped fresh mint

1 onion, finely chopped

2 ounces feta cheese

Place the watermelon in a bowl and stir in the mint and onion. When ready to serve, drain off the excess juice. Sprinkle with the feta.

OPTIONAL: Serve drizzled with Caramelized Balsamic Vinegar (page 6).

Green Bean Salad

SERVES 4 TO 6

8 ounces green beans

2 large vine-ripened tomatoes, chopped

2 ounces walnuts, chopped

¼ cup balsamic vinegar

Put the beans in a microwaveable bowl with ¼ cup water. Microwave for 4 minutes, or until just tender. Drain and place on a serving plate. Top with the tomatoes, sprinkle with the walnuts, and drizzle with the vinegar.

OPTIONAL: Caramelized Balsamic Vinegar (page 6) is really nice, too.

Pea & Mint Salad

SERVES 4

2 cups snow peas

2 tablespoons chopped fresh mint

7 tablespoons crumbled feta cheese

2 tablespoons fresh lemon juice

Place the snow peas in a bowl and cover with boiling water. Let sit for 2 minutes. Drain and rinse under cold water; pat dry. In a serving bowl, combine the snow peas, mint, and feta. Drizzle with the lemon juice and toss gently to combine.

Potato Salad

SERVES 4

A recipe from the ever-helpful Cathy DiBella . . . Yuuuuummy!

8 red potatoes, cut into chunks

7 tablespoons sour cream

6 tablespoons GF mayonnaise

1 tablespoon GF whole-grain mustard

In a saucepan of boiling water, cook the potatoes for 8 minutes, or until soft when pierced. Drain and let cool. In a bowl, combine the remaining ingredients and chill. Toss the potatoes with the salad dressing when ready to serve.

OPTIONAL: Add some finely diced celery, scallions, or whatever vegetables you have into the mix.

Roast Butternut Squash & Fig Salad

SERVES 4

Recipe by the lovely Carolyn Thomson.

4-ounce piece peeled butternut squash, sliced and roasted

4 ounces dried figs, quartered

4 ounces baby spinach

2 ounces walnuts, chopped

Arrange the roasted squash and figs on a bed of spinach and sprinkle with the walnuts.

OPTIONAL: Drizzle generously with Caramelized Balsamic Vinegar (page 6). Mmmmm!

Summer Salad

SERVES 4

A little beauty created by Rachael to get Jaxson to eat salad!

4 ounces mixed greens

1 pint strawberries, quartered

2 ounces snow peas

2 mangoes

In a salad bowl, combine the greens, strawberries, and snow peas. Cut the mangoes off the pits. Slice the flesh and add to the salad. Squeeze the juice from around the mango pits over the top of the salad, lightly tossing to coat.

Sweet Salad

SERVES 4

A recipe by Chef Dan Primmer.

1 pound sweet potatoes, peeled and diced

Kernels from 2 large ears of corn

6 tablespoons honey

½ cup plain Greek yogurt

Preheat the oven to 325°F. Line a baking sheet with parchment paper. In a bowl, toss together the sweet potato, corn, and honey. Arrange on the baking sheet and bake for 10 minutes, or until the sweet potato is soft. Let cool. To serve, toss the vegetables with the yogurt.

Waldorf Salad

SERVES 4

4 cups diced apples

¾ cup raisins

2 ounces pecans, chopped

½ cup GF mayonnaise

In a bowl, combine all the ingredients. Refrigerate until ready to serve.

Watermelon Salad

SERVES 4

About 2 pounds seedless watermelon, cubed

½ bunch watercress

Mint leaves from 6 sprigs, chopped

2 tablespoons fresh lemon juice

In a bowl, combine the watermelon, watercress, and mint, tossing lightly. Drizzle with the lemon juice and toss again.

NOTE: Ninety percent of a watermelon is (you guessed it) water, so it is a great hydrator for children in those warm summer months.

POTATOES, RICE & BEANS

Baked Lemon Potatoes

SERVES 4

A recipe from Michelle Dodd. These are sensational!

4 medium potatoes

3 tablespoons olive oil

1 tablespoon butter

½ cup fresh lemon juice

Preheat the oven to 350°F. Peel the potatoes and cut into eighths. In a pot of boiling water, parboil the potatoes for 3 minutes. Heat the oil, butter, and lemon juice in a baking dish in the oven. Toss the potatoes in the pan, basting with the oil mixture, and bake for 15 to 20 minutes, or until golden.

OPTIONAL: Add crushed garlic to the oil, butter, and lemon juice. Garlic is a powerful antibiotic, and when used on a regular basis, it can improve the immune system and help ward off colds and flu.

Baked Rice

SERVES 4

2 tablespoons butter, melted

1 cup rice

2 cups GF beef stock

2 ounces Parmesan cheese, grated

Preheat the oven to 350°F. Coat a baking dish with the butter. Add the rice and pour the stock over it. Sprinkle with the Parmesan, cover, and bake for 45 minutes.

Bombay Potatoes

SERVES 6

10 small potatoes, cut in half

2 cans (14.5 ounces each) chopped tomatoes

2 tablespoons GF garam masala

½ cup plain yogurt

Preheat the oven to 350°F. Line a large baking dish with parchment paper. Place the potatoes in the dish. In a bowl, mix the tomatoes with the garam masala. Pour the mixture over the potatoes and bake for 40 to 45 minutes, or until the potatoes are tender. Serve dolloped with the yogurt.

Butter Bean & Potato Puree

SERVES 4

8 ounces potatoes, peeled

1 can (15.5 ounces) butter beans

2 cloves garlic, crushed

¼ cup light cream

In a large pot, combine the potatoes and beans and cover with water. Bring to a boil and cook for 15 minutes, or until the potatoes are tender. Drain and mash to a puree. Add the garlic and cream and stir until creamy and smooth.

OPTIONAL: Add 2 tablespoons chopped parsley.

Coconut Rice

SERVES 4

1¼ cups basmati rice

2 cans (13.5 ounces each) coconut milk

¾ cup raisins

In a large pot, combine the rice, coconut milk, and 2 cups water and bring to a boil over high heat. Reduce the heat to low, add the raisins, cover, and simmer for 25 minutes, or until the liquid is absorbed and the rice is tender. Stir often.

OPTIONAL: Add a pinch of turmeric for color.

Crispy Parmesan Wedges

SERVES 4

4 medium potatoes, cut into wedges

½ cup olive oil

2 ounces Parmesan cheese, grated

2 tablespoons thyme leaves

Preheat the oven to 350°F. Place the potato wedges in a baking dish, brush with the oil, and toss to coat. Bake for 20 minutes. Sprinkle with the Parmesan and thyme. Bake for 10 to 15 minutes more, or until the potatoes are crisp outside and tender inside. Do not turn the potatoes during baking.

Crunchy Wedges

SERVES 5

These are gooooooooooooooood!

2 large potatoes

⅓ cup olive oil

2 cups GF cornflakes, crushed

1 tablespoon herb seasoning

Preheat the oven to 400°F. Line a baking sheet with parchment paper. Cut the potatoes into wedges and place in a large bowl. Drizzle the oil over the potatoes until all the wedges are covered. In a shallow bowl, mix the cornflakes and herb seasoning. Coat the potatoes generously in the cornflake mixture and place on the baking sheet. Roast for 20 minutes, then flip over and roast for 15 minutes more.

OPTIONAL: This can also be made with sweet potatoes. Add Parmesan cheese and paprika for an extra zing. Yum!!

Fried Rice

SERVES 2

S.c.r.u.m.p.t.i.o.u.s!

1 cup brown rice

2 slices bacon, diced

1 egg

¼ cup GF tamari sauce

In a saucepan, cook the rice according to package directions. Meanwhile, in a skillet, cook the bacon until crisp. Pour off all but a skim of fat. Crack the egg into the skillet, breaking the yolk to ensure spreading. Rinse the rice under hot water, stirring it to separate. Drain thoroughly, add to the bacon and egg, cover evenly with the tamari sauce, and toss well to heat through.

OPTIONAL: Also nice with diced pepper, pineapple, peas, chopped scallions, or corn and 1 teaspoon of GF sweet chili sauce.

Garlic Potatoes

SERVES 4

4 large potatoes, peeled and cut into ½-inch slices

4 ounces mozzarella cheese, shredded

2 cloves garlic, crushed through a press

1 cup sour cream

Preheat the oven to 350°F. In a vegetable steamer, cook the potatoes for 10 minutes, or until just soft. Set aside. In a bowl, combine all but ½ cup of the mozzarella, the garlic, and the sour cream. In a 10-inch square baking dish, alternate layers of potatoes with the sour cream mixture, ending with the sour cream. Top with the reserved ½ cup mozzarella and bake for 30 to 40 minutes.

Healthy Rustic Fries

SERVES 4

4 medium potatoes

1 tablespoon olive oil

Preheat the oven to 425°F. Cut the potatoes into ¾-inch-thick sticks. In a large pot of boiling water, cook them until just tender. Drain well and pat completely dry with paper towels. In a large bowl, toss the potatoes with the oil and season with sea salt. Arrange in a single layer on a baking sheet. Roast for 25 minutes, or until browned.

OPTIONAL: Add a pinch of paprika before baking.

Home-Style Beans

SERVES 4 TO 6

2 tablespoons olive oil

1 large yellow bell pepper, chopped

2 cans (15 ounces each) white kidney beans

1 can (28 ounces) crushed tomatoes with herbs and garlic

In a medium saucepan, heat the oil. Add the bell pepper and cook until just soft. Add the beans, tomatoes, and sea salt and pepper to taste. Simmer for 20 minutes over low heat, stirring occasionally.

Mashed Potatoes

SERVES 4

4 potatoes, peeled and cubed

1 clove garlic, crushed through a press

2 tablespoons butter

½ cup milk

In a pot of boiling water, cook the potatoes for 5 minutes, or until soft. Drain and return to the pot. Add the remaining ingredients and mash until smooth. Season with sea salt and pepper to taste.

TIP: Waxy potatoes such as Yukon Gold are recommended for smooth, creamy mashed potatoes.

Potato Pancakes

MAKES 10

A recipe by Carol Logan.

2 cups mashed potatoes

2 cups cooked diced bacon

½ cup chopped scallions

1 envelope (1.4 ounces) GF creamy chicken and vegetable soup mix

Mix all the ingredients together and form into patties. In a lightly oiled nonstick skillet, cook until browned on both sides.

Potato Scallops

SERVES 4

4 large potatoes

2 cups GF self-rising flour, plus more for coating

¾ cup sunflower oil

Peel and wash the potatoes. Thinly slice and pat dry. Sift the flour into a bowl and season with sea salt and pepper to taste. Make a well in the center and gradually add 1 cup water to make a thick batter, beating until free of lumps. Coat the potato slices lightly with extra flour, shaking off the excess. In a large pan, heat the oil until very hot. Working in batches, dip each potato slice into the batter, letting the excess drip off. Add the potatoes to the hot oil and cook until lightly golden. Drain on paper towels and sprinkle with sea salt.

Puffed Sweet Potato

SERVES 4

½ cup milk

2 tablespoons butter, melted

2 cups mashed sweet potato

1 egg, separated

Preheat the oven to 350°F. In a small bowl, stir together the milk and 1 tablespoon of the melted butter. Season generously with salt and pepper. In a bowl, beat the sweet potato with the milk mixture and egg yolk. Beat the egg white until stiff peaks form and fold into the mixture. Use the remaining 1 tablespoon melted butter to grease a 12-cup mini muffin tin. Dollop the mixture into the cups and bake for 25 minutes.

Rice Pilaf

SERVES 4

A recipe from the lovely Fleur Whelligan.

1 onion, diced

2 cloves garlic, chopped

1 cup basmati rice

2 cups GF vegetable stock

Preheat the oven to 350°F. In a nonstick skillet, cook the onion in a little water. Add the garlic and rice and stir. Add the stock and bring to a boil. Transfer the mixture to an 8-inch square baking dish, cover, and bake for 30 minutes. Remove from the oven and fluff the rice with a fork.

OPTIONAL: Stir in a knob of butter and some chopped parsley.

Rosemary & Thyme Roasted Spuds

SERVES 6

5 large potatoes, peeled and cut into thick wedges

¼ cup olive oil

Rosemary leaves from 8 sprigs

Thyme leaves from 8 sprigs

Preheat the oven to 400°F. On a rimmed baking sheet, toss the potatoes with the oil and fresh herbs. Sprinkle with some sea salt if desired. Roast for 35 to 40 minutes, turning to ensure that the wedges brown evenly.

Tennessee Taters

SERVES 4

4 potatoes

2 teaspoons butter

1 cup shredded Cheddar cheese

4 slices bacon, diced and cooked until crisp

Preheat the oven to 350°F. Pierce the potatoes several times, wrap each in foil, and bake for 40 minutes, or until fork-tender. Cut a large crisscross in the top of each. Push the potato toward the center so the split opens wide. Place ½ teaspoon butter and ¼ cup Cheddar in each, pushing down firmly. Sprinkle with the bacon and run under the broiler to melt the cheese.

VEGETABLES

Aglio Broccoli

SERVES 4

1 large bunch broccoli

2 tablespoons olive oil

2 tablespoons butter

2 cloves garlic, crushed
through a press

Cut the broccoli into chunky pieces, including about 1½ inches of the stalk. Cook in a vegetable steamer for about 8 minutes. Remove and run under cold water. In a nonstick skillet, heat the oil and butter over medium heat. Add the garlic and cook until it just begins to toast (be careful not to burn it). Add the broccoli and turn gently until well coated and warm.

NOTE: *Aglio* means "garlic" in Italian.

Asparagus with Butter & Parmesan

SERVES 4

2 bunches asparagus

1 tablespoon butter, melted

2 ounces Parmesan cheese,
shaved

Bring water to a boil in a large skillet. Add the asparagus, return to a boil, then drain. Drizzle with the butter and Parmesan. Season with sea salt and pepper to taste.

Baked Onions

SERVES 4

4 onions

1 tablespoon olive oil

½ cup GF vegetable stock

Preheat the oven to 300°F. Cut the ends off the onions but do not peel them. Place them in a roasting pan and brush with the oil. Pour the stock into the pan, then bake for 1½ hours, or until they are soft when gently squeezed. Place the onions on a serving dish and, with a sharp knife, gently cut a crisscross into the top of each onion. Peel back the skins and sprinkle black pepper on the tops to serve.

Fried Brussels Sprouts

SERVES 4

16 brussels sprouts

4 slices bacon, diced

1 tablespoon butter

2 tablespoons chopped walnuts

Cut a crisscross into the base of the sprouts. In a pot of boiling water, cook the sprouts for 8 minutes, or until tender. In a skillet, cook the bacon until crisp. Add the cooked sprouts, butter, and walnuts to the skillet and cook for 2 minutes.

OPTIONAL: Make this with cauliflower instead of brussels sprouts.

TIP: Brussels sprouts team nicely with a glaze of butter and a sprinkling of chopped nuts and sage. Some black pepper and nutmeg won't hurt, either.

Garlic Mushrooms

SERVES 4

1 pound button mushrooms

2 tablespoons olive oil

1 or 2 cloves garlic, crushed through a press

6 sprigs flat-leaf parsley, chopped

Preheat the oven to 350°F. Place the mushrooms in a large baking dish. Toss with the oil and garlic. Bake for 15 minutes, or until the mushrooms are tender and lightly browned. Stir in the parsley.

NOTE: Cook close to serving.

Green Beans & Pine Nuts

SERVES 4

These are scrumptious!

8 ounces green beans

3 tablespoons olive oil

¼ cup pine nuts

Put the beans in a microwaveable bowl with ¼ cup water and cook for 40 seconds, or until crisp-tender; then drain. In a small nonstick skillet, heat the oil over low heat. Add the beans and cook for 1 minute. Add the pine nuts, stirring until heated through and lightly toasted.

Herbed Zucchini

SERVES 4

3 zucchini, cut on the diagonal into thick slices

1 tablespoon butter

1 tablespoon finely chopped parsley

In a pot of boiling salted water, cook the zucchini for 3 minutes. Drain well. In a saucepan, heat the butter. Add the zucchini, season well with sea salt and pepper, and cook over low heat, stirring occasionally, until golden brown. Sprinkle with the parsley.

Honey & Mustard Roast Parsnips

SERVES 6

2¼ pounds parsnips, quartered lengthwise

¼ cup olive oil

3 tablespoons honey

4 tablespoons GF whole-grain mustard

Preheat the oven to 400°F. In a pot of lightly salted water, cook the parsnips for 5 minutes. Put the oil in a large roasting pan and place in the oven to heat. Drain the parsnips and add to the hot oil, tossing to coat well. Roast for 30 minutes, or until crispy. Meanwhile, mix the honey and mustard. Pour over the parsnips and roast 5 minutes longer.

Honey Sesame Carrots

SERVES 4

6 carrots, peeled and cut into rounds

1 tablespoon butter

1 tablespoon honey

2 tablespoons sesame seeds

In a saucepan of boiling water, cook the carrots for 4 to 5 minutes, or until they are just tender. Drain and return to the pan. Add the butter and honey and sauté. Add the sesame seeds just as the carrots are starting to brown.

Peas with Mint & Garlic Butter

SERVES 4 TO 6

1 pound frozen peas

1 tablespoon butter

1 clove garlic, crushed through a press

8 fresh mint leaves, chopped

Cook the peas according to package directions. Drain and return to the pan. Add the butter, garlic, and sea salt and pepper to taste. Serve sprinkled with the mint.

Roasted Beets

SERVES 4

¼ cup olive oil

¼ cup balsamic vinegar

Basil leaves from 4 sprigs, chopped

4 beets, peeled and quartered

Preheat the oven to 350°F. In a bowl, mix together the oil, vinegar, and basil. Place the beet wedges in a baking dish and drizzle with the dressing. Roast for 30 to 35 minutes, or until tender.

Roasted Corn with Parmesan & Cayenne

SERVES 4

4 ears corn

2 tablespoons GF mayonnaise

2 tablespoons grated Parmesan cheese

½ teaspoon cayenne pepper

Preheat the oven to 350°F. Place the unhusked corn directly on the oven rack and bake for 20 minutes, or until the corn is soft when you press on it. Peel the husks back, but do not pull off. Remove the corn silk and tie each husk together with a piece of husk so you can hold on to it like a handle. Preheat a grill or the broiler. Grill or broil the corn for 6 minutes, or until the kernels are slightly blackened all around and start popping. Rub the corn with the mayonnaise and sprinkle evenly with the Parmesan and cayenne pepper.

OPTIONAL: Serve with lime wedges.

Sautéed Cherry Tomatoes

SERVES 4 TO 6

2 tablespoons butter

8 ounces cherry tomatoes

2 tablespoons fresh thyme leaves

In a nonstick skillet, melt the butter over medium heat. Add the tomatoes and thyme and season generously with sea salt and pepper. Cook for 5 minutes, or until the tomatoes begin to soften.

Spicy Pumpkin Wedges

SERVES 4

1 pound pumpkin, peeled and cut into 4 wedges

2 tablespoons olive oil

1 teaspoon ground cumin

1 teaspoon grated nutmeg

Preheat the oven to 350°F. On a rimmed baking sheet, toss the pumpkin with the oil. Sprinkle with the cumin and nutmeg, and season to taste with sea salt and pepper. Toss to coat. Bake for 30 minutes, or until tender, turning halfway through the cooking.

Spinach with Lemon

SERVES 4

This is a really nice way to eat spinach!

1 bunch fresh spinach, shredded

2 tablespoons butter, at room temperature

2 tablespoons fresh lemon juice

In a pot of boiling water, cook the spinach for 5 minutes, or until wilted. Drain well and return to the dry saucepan. Season with sea salt and pepper to taste. Add the butter and lemon juice and toss together.

Stumpot

SERVES 2

A Dutch classic from the lovely Lani Smith.

2 potatoes, chopped

2 carrots, chopped

1 large yellow onion, chopped

2 cups GF chicken or vegetable stock

In a large saucepan, combine all the ingredients plus pepper to taste. Bring to a boil. Reduce to a simmer and cook for 6 to 8 minutes, or until the vegetables are soft. Drain off the excess liquid and mash.

Veggie Kebabs

MAKES 16

The word "kebab" is Arabic and means "a dish of meat roasted or grilled on a skewer."

1 red bell pepper, cut into large chunks

1 Spanish onion, cut into large chunks

¼ fresh pineapple, peeled and cut into large chunks

8 large mushrooms, halved

Preheat the grill. Thread the ingredients, alternating them, onto soaked bamboo skewers. Grill for a couple of minutes on each side, until soft and warm.

MAINS

Those that know, do. Those that understand, teach.

—Aristotle

BEEF

BBQ Beef Stir-fry

SERVES 4

Serve the beef on top of a salad—even just shredded iceberg lettuce is nice.

1 pound beef, cut for stir-fry

⅔ cup GF barbecue sauce

2 tablespoons sesame oil

4 scallions, cut lengthwise into thin strips

In a bowl, combine the beef and barbecue sauce; let stand for 15 minutes. In a wok or nonstick skillet, heat the sesame oil. Working in batches, stir-fry the beef for 1 minute, or until cooked on the outside and medium on the inside. Remove from the pan. Add the scallions to the pan and quickly stir-fry. Add to the beef.

HOW TO COOK STIR-FRIES: Chop the ingredients into equal-size pieces so they will cook evenly. If you have the time, marinate the meat for at least 2 hours for the flavors to develop. But if you don't have time, even 15 minutes will improve the taste. Make sure any oil used is very hot before adding the other ingredients. First, add veggies that take longer to cook (carrots, onions); after 2 minutes, add the other veggies (snow peas, bell pepper); when the stir-fry is almost done, add leafy greens and herbs.

Beef Casserole

SERVES 4

1 pound lean ground beef

1 large yellow onion, chopped

4 ounces cabbage, shredded

1 can (10.75 ounces) GF condensed tomato soup

Preheat the oven to 350°F. In a nonstick skillet, brown the beef and onion. Drain and season with sea salt and pepper to taste. Spread over the bottom of a baking dish. Top with the cabbage. Pour the tomato soup on top, cover, and bake for 1 hour.

Beef Stroganoff

SERVES 4

Recipe from Glen Turnbull.

1 pound beef, cut for stir-fry

1 envelope (1 ounce) GF beef Stroganoff seasoning

4 ounces cream cheese, at room temperature

8 ounces mushrooms, sliced

In a nonstick skillet, lightly fry the beef strips. Add the seasoning mix and ½ cup water and simmer until tender. Add the cream cheese and stir until melted. Add the mushrooms and simmer for 5 minutes, or until the mushrooms soften.

NOTE: Don't cook meat straight from the refrigerator. It will be far more tender if you let it come to room temperature first.

Coffee & Pepper–Crusted Steaks

SERVES 4

This is charmingly unusual!

2 tablespoons coffee beans

2 tablespoons black peppercorns

4 steaks, ¾ inch to 1¼ inches thick

Preheat the broiler or grill to high. In a coffee or spice grinder, coarsely grind the coffee beans and peppercorns. Press the mixture evenly onto both sides of the steaks. Coat the steaks lightly with cooking spray. Broil or grill the steaks for 8 to 10 minutes, turning once halfway through the grilling time (do not turn the steaks until you see beads of juice on the surface). Remove the steaks from the grill and season both sides with sea salt. Let rest for 3 minutes before serving.

NOTE: Have you ever wondered how long you should cook your steak? Try these cooking times recommended by Chef Peter Wolf from the Eumundi Market, located on Australia's Sunshine Coast. (Times are based on a 1-inch-thick steak cooked on a hot grill.)
Well done: 5 minutes each side
Medium: 3 minutes each side
Rare: 2 minutes each side

Corned Beef

SERVES 6

2¼ pounds corned beef

10 whole cloves

⅓ cup pure maple syrup

Place the meat in a large pot and cover with water. Bring to a boil. Reduce the heat and cook for 1 hour, or until tender. Preheat the oven to 350°F. Place the meat in a shallow baking dish, press the cloves into the meat, drizzle with the syrup, and dust with freshly cracked pepper. Bake for 15 minutes. Slice the meat across the grain to serve.

Harch Steak

SERVES 2

Recipe by Karen Harch.

3 tablespoons GF ketchup

3 tablespoons GF barbecue sauce

1 tablespoon GF Worcestershire sauce

2 steaks

Preheat the oven to 375°F. In a bowl, combine the ketchup, barbecue sauce, and Worcestershire sauce. Place the steaks in a baking dish and pour the sauce over the meat. Cover and cook for 1 hour, or until the meat is tender.

Massaman Curry

SERVES 4

Y.U.M.M.Y!!!

1 pound lean beef, cut for stir-fry

1 tablespoon GF massaman curry paste

1¾ cups coconut cream

3 red potatoes, peeled and cubed

In a nonstick skillet or Dutch oven, cook the beef with 2 tablespoons water over high heat until browned on the outside. In a small bowl, combine the massaman curry paste and coconut cream and add to the beef. Add the potatoes, reduce to the very lowest heat, and simmer for 30 minutes, or until the potatoes are tender.

OPTIONAL: Add ½ cup cashews and serve with rice.

Mustard Roast Beef

SERVES 4

Serve with your favorite roast veggies and GF gravy.

2¼ pounds prime roasting beef

¼ cup GF whole-grain mustard

3 tablespoons olive oil

Preheat the oven to 265°F. Place the beef in a roasting pan and glaze with the mustard. Drizzle with the oil and bake for 3 hours. (Cooking it for this time will ensure that the beef is well done but still very tender!) Turn the roast over halfway through the cooking time.

Pesto-Stuffed Steaks

SERVES 4

2 beef rib-eye steaks (about 1¼ inches thick)

¼ cup GF basil pesto

3 tablespoons grated Parmesan cheese

1 tablespoon olive oil

Preheat a heavy frying pan until it is hot. Cut into the side of each steak, forming a deep pocket (do not cut through). Mix the pesto and Parmesan and spread in the pockets. Press closed and drizzle the steaks with the oil. Place the steaks carefully in the pan and cook for 6 to 8 minutes for a medium steak, turning over when you see juices on the surface. When done to your liking, remove, cover, and let stand for 5 to 10 minutes. Cut the beef into thick strips to serve.

Quick Meat Loaf

SERVES 4

Serve hot with vegetables, salad, or mashed potatoes.

1 pound ground sirloin

3 eggs, lightly beaten

¾ cup GF bread crumbs

¼ cup tomato paste

Preheat the oven to 350°F. Line a 9 by 5 by 3-inch loaf pan with parchment paper or foil. In a large bowl, combine the beef, eggs, bread crumbs, and 3 tablespoons of the tomato paste. Put into the loaf pan. Spread the remaining 1 tablespoon tomato paste on top of the meat loaf. Bake for 50 minutes, or until lightly browned on top.

OPTIONAL: For a Mexican meat loaf, omit the tomato paste and reduce the eggs to 2. Use a 16-ounce jar of GF picante taco sauce. Use three-quarters of the sauce in the loaf and the rest to coat.

TIP: This is also great to freeze.

Rissoles

SERVES 4

8 ounces ground beef

1 onion, finely chopped

3 tablespoons sweet chili sauce

1 egg, lightly beaten

Put all the ingredients into a bowl and season with pepper. Using your hands, mix together well. Divide the mixture into 8 portions and shape into 8 balls, flattening each slightly. In a nonstick skillet over medium heat, fry the rissoles for 3 to 4 minutes on each side, or until golden brown and firm.

OPTIONAL: If the mixture seems too wet, add ½ cup bread crumbs before rolling into balls.

Shepherd's Pie

SERVES 6

A recipe inspired by the Gippsland Harvest Festival, Victoria.

1 pound lean ground beef

⅔ cup GF fruit chutney

6 potatoes, boiled and mashed

¾ cup shredded Cheddar cheese

Preheat the oven to 350°F. In a nonstick skillet, brown the beef, seasoning it with sea salt and pepper to taste. Mix in the chutney. Pour into a 13 by 9-inch baking dish, top with an even layer of mashed potatoes, and sprinkle with the Cheddar. Bake for 20 to 30 minutes, or until the cheese is nice and bubbly.

OPTIONAL: Slice a tomato or two over the beef mixture before topping with the mashed potatoes.

Soy Steaks

SERVES 4

Recipe by Brian Boholt. Serve with a crisp, fresh salad.

¼ cup GF soy sauce

1 tablespoon light brown sugar

1 clove garlic, crushed through a press

4 rib-eye steaks

In a shallow container big enough to hold the steaks, mix together the soy sauce, brown sugar, and garlic. Marinate the steaks in the mixture for 3 hours. Broil or grill the steaks for 3 to 4 minutes per side, or until done to your liking.

Steak Burgundy

SERVES 2

A recipe from Paul at the Buderim Butchers, Queensland, Australia. Serve with roast vegetables or salad. Yum. Yum. Yum!

2 good-size boneless rib steaks

1 cup red wine

2 teaspoons butter

2 cloves garlic, crushed through a press

Marinate the steaks in the wine for 2 hours. Preheat the oven to 350°F. Cut 2 pieces of foil big enough to make a packet to enclose the steaks individually. In a small bowl, mix together the butter and garlic. Place a steak in the center of a piece of foil and top with a dollop of garlic butter. Bring two sides of the foil together and fold to seal. Seal the ends. Place the steaks on a baking sheet and bake for 45 minutes.

Steak with Mushroom Ragout

SERVES 4

*Serve with boiled potatoes or creamy polenta
and green beans. Delicious!*

4 round steaks (7 ounces each)

2 tablespoons butter, at room temperature

4 ounces mushrooms, sliced

½ cup heavy cream

Brush the steaks with 1 tablespoon of the butter. Preheat a large nonstick skillet over medium-high heat. Add the steaks and cook, without turning, until moisture appears (3 to 4 minutes). Turn and cook for 3 to 4 minutes more, for medium. Transfer the steaks to a plate, cover with foil, and let rest for 5 minutes. Meanwhile, in the same skillet, melt the remaining 1 tablespoon butter. Add the mushrooms and cook until softened. Add the cream and simmer until reduced and thickened. Season with sea salt and pepper to taste. Pour the mushroom sauce over the steaks and serve.

Veal Steaks with Creamy Pepper Sauce

SERVES 4

4 veal steaks

1 tablespoon lemon pepper

⅓ cup marinated roasted red peppers, drained and pureed

¾ cup heavy cream

Broil the veal steaks to your liking. Cover with foil. In a nonstick skillet, combine the remaining ingredients and simmer until the mixture thickens. Serve the sauce generously drizzled over the veal.

Veal with Olives

SERVES 4

4 veal cutlets, pounded paper thin

¼ cup butter

⅓ cup Marsala wine

10 pitted green olives, sliced

Sprinkle the veal with sea salt and pepper. In a large skillet, melt the butter. Add the veal and brown lightly on both sides. Add the Marsala and olives and heat for 1 minute.

CHICKEN

Creativity is allowing yourself to make mistakes.
Art is knowing which ones to keep.
—Scott Adams

Apricot-Glazed Chicken

SERVES 2

2 skinless, boneless chicken breast halves (6 ounces each)

1 cup apricot preserves

2 teaspoons GF Dijon mustard

5 drops GF hot sauce

Preheat the oven to 400°F. Place the chicken in a baking dish. In a small bowl, mix together the preserves, mustard, and hot sauce. Spoon the mixture over the chicken. Bake for 15 minutes. Baste with the pan drippings and bake for 10 minutes longer.

Bacon-Wrapped Chicken

SERVES 6

6 skinless, boneless chicken breast halves (6 ounces each)

8 ounces cream cheese with onions and chives

1 tablespoon butter

6 slices bacon

Preheat the oven to 350°F. Grease a baking sheet. Pound the chicken to a ½-inch thickness. Spread 2 generous tablespoons cream cheese over each cutlet. Dot each with ½ teaspoon butter and season with sea salt and pepper to taste. Roll up each cutlet and wrap each roll with a slice of bacon. Place seam side down on the baking sheet and bake for 20 minutes, or until the juices run clear.

Cheese & Ham Chicken Rolls

SERVES 2

- 2 skinless, boneless chicken breast halves (6 ounces each)
- 1 tablespoon GF whole-grain mustard
- 2 slices Swiss cheese
- 2 slices baked ham

Preheat the oven to 350°F. Pound the chicken flat. Smear with the mustard. Lay a slice of cheese and ham on each piece of chicken. Roll up and secure with a toothpick. Bake for 20 minutes, or until browned and cooked through. Remove the toothpick and slice the roll into rounds to serve.

Chicken, Butternut Squash & Chickpea Curry

SERVES 6

In the words of Wendy Beattie, "This is fabulous!" Serve with steamed rice.

- 1½-pound butternut squash
- 6 boneless, skinless chicken thighs
- 1 can (15 ounces) chickpeas, rinsed and drained
- 1 jar (15 ounces) GF korma curry sauce

Halve and seed the squash. In a vegetable steamer, cook for 5 to 10 minutes, or until almost cooked. Let cool, then peel and cut into cubes. Halve the chicken thighs. In a saucepan, combine the chicken, squash, and chickpeas. Pour in the korma sauce, then wash out the jar with ¼ cup hot water and add to the saucepan. Cover and cook over medium heat for about 30 minutes, or until the chicken is cooked through.

OPTIONAL: Garnish with cilantro. Replace the water with coconut cream.

Chicken Marsala

SERVES 4

Sensational! Serve this easy dish with mashed potatoes or rice and seasonal vegetables.

4 skinless, boneless chicken breast halves (6 ounces each)

8 ounces mushrooms, sliced

½ cup Marsala wine

¾ cup heavy cream

Pound the chicken lightly, then cut into strips. In a large nonstick skillet, cook the chicken for 8 minutes, or until cooked through and the juices run clear. Add the mushrooms and cook until softened. Add the Marsala, bring to a boil, and cook for 3 minutes, seasoning with sea salt and pepper to taste. Stir in the cream and simmer for 5 minutes to heat through.

Chicken Tikka Masala

SERVES 4

You will cook this again and again and again! Serve with rice.

1¼ pounds boneless, skinless chicken breasts, cut into chunks

2 tablespoons GF tikka masala paste

1 can (10.75 ounces) GF condensed tomato soup

3 tablespoons plain yogurt

Preheat a nonstick skillet. Add the chicken and cook for 5 to 6 minutes, or until browned. Add the tikka masala paste and soup and simmer for 15 minutes. Stir in the yogurt and heat through.

Chutney Chicken Dish

SERVES 2

This is deliciously simple! Serve with rice or vegetables.

- 2 tablespoons GF fruit chutney
- 2 tablespoons GF Dijon mustard
- 2 boneless, skinless chicken breast halves (6 ounces each)
- ¼ cup shredded Cheddar cheese

Preheat the oven to 350°F. In a small bowl, combine the chutney and mustard. Spread the mixture over the chicken breasts. Put the chicken in a baking dish and cover with the Cheddar. Bake for 15 to 20 minutes, or until the juices run clear.

Green Chicken Curry

SERVES 4

A ripper recipe from Shane McCosker.

- ¼ cup GF green curry paste
- 4 boneless, skinless chicken thighs, cut into strips
- 1 can (14 ounces) coconut cream
- 4 ounces green beans, cut into 2-inch pieces

Preheat a wok or large skillet over medium heat. Put in the green curry paste and cook, stirring, for 1 minute or so, until fragrant. Add the chicken and cook, stirring, for about 10 minutes, or until almost cooked through. Stir in the coconut cream and bring to a boil. Simmer for 30 minutes. Ten minutes before the curry is done, add the beans.

OPTIONAL: We often add more vegetables.

Indian Chicken Curry

SERVES 4

Very easy and very yummy! Serve with rice.

1 rotisserie chicken

1 cup plain yogurt

6 tablespoons GF mayonnaise

2 tablespoons GF curry powder

Remove the skin and pull the meat off the bones of the chicken. Chop the meat into bite-size pieces. In a large bowl, mix together the yogurt, mayonnaise, and curry powder. Add the chicken to the yogurt mixture and toss to coat. Marinate for at least 1 hour. Preheat the oven to 350°F. Spoon the chicken into a baking dish and bake for 20 to 25 minutes, until heated through.

OPTIONAL: Garnish with cilantro and lemon wedges.

Italian Chicken

SERVES 4

This is sooooooooooooooo good!!!

1½ pounds boneless, skinless chicken breasts, cut into thickish strips

1 can (14.5 ounces) diced tomatoes with basil and onion

2 ounces pitted kalamata olives

4 ounces grated mozzarella cheese

Preheat the oven to 350°F. Arrange the chicken in a baking dish big enough to hold it snugly in one layer. Mix together the tomatoes and olives and pour over the chicken. Sprinkle with the mozzarella. Bake for 20 minutes, or until the chicken is cooked through and the juices run clear.

OPTIONAL: Substitute your favorite GF pasta sauce for the tomatoes.

Mango Chicken

SERVES 4

Serve with steamed rice and vegetables.

⅔ cup GF mango chutney

1 tablespoon GF Dijon mustard

½ bunch cilantro, chopped, plus more for garnish

1¼ pounds boneless, skinless chicken breasts, cut into thickish strips

Preheat the oven to 400°F. Line a baking sheet with parchment paper. In a bowl, combine the chutney, mustard, and ½ bunch cilantro. Add the chicken and coat well with the chutney mix. Place on the baking sheet and bake for 15 to 20 minutes, or until cooked through. Garnish with the additional cilantro.

Soy Chicken

SERVES 4 TO 6

2¼ pounds bone-in chicken parts

½ cup packed light brown sugar

½ cup GF soy sauce

1 tablespoon butter

Preheat the oven to 350°F. Place the chicken skin side down in a baking dish. In a small saucepan, combine the remaining ingredients and place over low heat until the butter is melted. Stir well to mix, then pour over the chicken. Bake for 20 minutes. Turn and bake for 20 minutes longer, basting occasionally.

Sticky Wings

MAKES A LOT!

A recipe from the charming Kimmy Morrison.

¼ cup honey

2 teaspoons GF curry powder

2 teaspoons GF soy sauce

4½ pounds chicken wings

Combine the honey, curry powder, and soy sauce. Place the chicken in an airtight container. Add the honey mixture, tossing to coat. Marinate overnight in the fridge. Cook the wings on a grill until cooked through, basting frequently. Or bake in the oven: Preheat the oven to 400°F. Put the wings on a parchment-lined baking sheet and bake for 15 minutes, then turn and baste. Bake for an additional 20 to 25 minutes, until golden brown.

Sweet & Spicy Chicken

SERVES 3

½ cup orange marmalade

1 to 2 teaspoons GF chili powder

6 chicken drumsticks

Preheat the oven to 350°F. Line a baking sheet with foil. Combine the marmalade and chili powder in a plastic sandwich bag. Add the chicken and shake until evenly coated. Place the chicken on the baking sheet and spoon on any remaining marmalade mixture. Bake for 30 to 40 minutes, or until cooked through.

Tangy Chicken Tenders

SERVES 4

1½ pounds boneless, skinless chicken breasts, cut into thickish strips

3 tablespoons GF all-purpose flour

1 cup GF barbecue sauce

½ cup orange juice

Preheat the oven to 350°F. Dredge the chicken strips in the flour. Coat a nonstick skillet with cooking spray and preheat. Add the chicken and cook until browned. Transfer the chicken to a shallow baking pan. Mix the barbecue sauce and orange juice and pour over the chicken. Cover and bake for 15 minutes. Uncover, baste with the sauce, and bake uncovered for 5 minutes longer.

Thai Chicken with Cucumber Noodles

SERVES 4

Recipe by Dan Primmer. This is just so tasty!

12 ounces boneless, skinless chicken breasts, cut into chunky pieces

½ cup GF sweet chili and ginger sauce

1 hothouse (seedless) cucumber

½ cup GF fried rice noodles (available in Asian markets)

In a nonstick skillet, cook the chicken in ¼ cup water until the water evaporates. Add the sweet chili sauce and simmer for 5 minutes, or until the chicken is cooked through. Remove from the heat. Thinly slice the cucumber lengthwise, then cut the slices into thin strips to resemble long, thin noodles. Add most of the cucumber slices and all the rice noodles to the chicken and mix gently. Serve topped with the remaining cucumber noodles as a garnish.

FISH & SHELLFISH

Only Robinson Crusoe had everything done by Friday!
—A parent

Baked Fish

SERVES 2

2 white fish fillets

1 teaspoon butter, melted

1 lemon, sliced

Preheat the oven to 350°F. Coat the fish with the butter and season with sea salt and pepper. Place the fish on a square of foil. Top with the lemon slices and close the packet. Bake for 20 minutes, or until the fish just flakes.

Baked Salmon with Pesto Crust

SERVES 4

A recipe from Michelle Dodd. This is fantastic!

4 salmon steaks

4 tablespoons GF basil pesto

2 ounces pecorino cheese, finely grated

1 lemon, halved

Preheat the oven to 350°F. Preheat an ovenproof skillet, put in the salmon steaks skin side down, and cook for 2 minutes to sear, then flip and cook on the second side for 2 minutes. Meanwhile, combine the pesto and pecorino. Spread the pesto mixture over the salmon steaks and squeeze fresh lemon juice over the top. Bake for 15 minutes.

Cheesy Fish Steaks

SERVES 4

4 fish steaks

¾ cup grated Monterey Jack cheese

1 teaspoon GF Worcestershire sauce

1 tablespoon milk

Preheat the broiler to medium. Broil the fish steaks for 5 minutes. Meanwhile, mix the remaining ingredients and season with sea salt and pepper to taste. Flip the fish and spread the uncooked side with the cheese mixture. Broil for 5 minutes, or until the fish is cooked through and the topping is bubbling.

OPTIONAL: Garnish with chopped fresh parsley.

Curried Fish with Coconut Rice

SERVES 4

This is a great way to make rice for a change!

1 can (14 ounces) coconut milk

1 cup jasmine rice

4 white fish fillets, cut into ¾-inch cubes

3 cups bottled GF korma curry sauce

In a saucepan, bring ½ cup water and the coconut milk to a boil. Add the rice and cook for 12 to 15 minutes, or until the rice is tender and the liquid has been absorbed. Meanwhile, in another saucepan, combine the fish and curry sauce. Bring to a boil and simmer for 5 minutes, or until the fish is cooked through. Divide the rice among serving plates and top with the fish mixture.

OPTIONAL: Garnish with cilantro.

Dukkah-Crusted Salmon

SERVES 4

Dukkah is a blend of roasted nuts, spices, and sesame seeds ground into a healthy condiment. It is Egyptian and is used in many Middle Eastern recipes.

4 skinless salmon fillets

⅓ cup dukkah

Preheat the oven to 300°F. Line a baking sheet with parchment paper. Place the salmon on the baking sheet. Lightly coat each fillet with olive oil cooking spray. Press the dukkah onto both sides of each fillet. Bake for 15 minutes.

Fish with Lemon Butter

SERVES 4

1 lemon

8 tablespoons (1 stick) butter, melted

3 sprigs parsley, chopped

4 fish fillets

Preheat the oven to 375°F. Grate 1 teaspoon lemon zest, then squeeze the lemon. In a small saucepan, bring the butter, lemon juice, zest, parsley, 1 teaspoon sea salt, and 1 teaspoon pepper to a boil. Reduce the heat and cook, stirring, for 10 minutes, or until thickened. Place the fish on a broiler pan or baking sheet. Pour half the butter sauce over the fish. Cover with foil and bake for 15 to 20 minutes. Serve with the remaining hot butter sauce poured over the fish.

OPTIONAL: Sprinkle the fish with a little lemon pepper before baking.

Fish with Mango & Kiwifruit

SERVES 2

4 white fish fillets

1 tablespoon butter, melted

2 kiwifruits, peeled and sliced

1 mango, sliced

Preheat a grill or a grill pan. Brush the fish with the butter and cook each side for 3 to 5 minutes, depending on thickness. In a skillet, heat the kiwifruits and mango. Serve layered on top of the fish.

Garlic Cream Shrimp

SERVES 4

1½ cups rice

½ cup heavy cream

2 cloves garlic, crushed through a press

16 jumbo shrimp, peeled and deveined

Cook the rice according to package directions, then rinse under hot water. Meanwhile, in a wok or nonstick skillet, combine the cream and garlic and simmer to reduce. Add the shrimp and cook until orange in color and warmed through. Serve on a bed of rice.

Herb-Crusted Fish

SERVES 4

Delicious served with lemon potatoes and a green salad.

4 white fish fillets

½ cup GF bread crumbs

3 sprigs fresh flat-leaf parsley, chopped

2 ounces Parmesan cheese, grated

Preheat the oven to 400°F. Place the fish on a foil-lined baking sheet. Combine the remaining ingredients and add sea salt and black pepper to taste. Sprinkle the bread crumb mixture over the fish and bake for 15 to 20 minutes, or until the fish just flakes.

Lime & Salmon Cakes

SERVES 6

A recipe from Jennette McCosker . . . Y.u.m.m.y!

Juice and grated zest of 1 lime

1 can (14.75 ounces) pink salmon, drained

1 egg

3 slices GF bread, grated into crumbs (see Note)

In a bowl, combine the lime juice, zest, salmon, egg, bread crumbs, and sea salt and pepper to taste. Mix well before shaping into 12 thick cakes. In a nonstick skillet, cook until firmed up and heated through.

NOTE: Fresh GF bread is easier to grate when frozen.

Oregano Fish

SERVES 4

Serve with salad. Recipe by Sue Edmondstone.

4 white fish fillets

2 tablespoons olive oil

Leaves from ½ bunch fresh oregano

2 cloves garlic, crushed through a press

Coat the fish with the oil, then sprinkle cracked pepper and the oregano over both sides of the fillets. Preheat a nonstick skillet over medium to high heat. Add the fish, sprinkle with the garlic, and cook for 1 to 2 minutes, or until golden. Flip and cook for 2 minutes longer.

Quick Mango Fish

SERVES 4

Serve with a lovely fresh green salad and a classic mustard-lemon vinaigrette.

4 pieces swordfish, mahimahi, or marlin

¼ cup olive oil

2 mangoes, sliced

Preheat a grill or grill pan to medium. Coat the fish liberally with the oil and cracked pepper. Grill until you can see the flesh turning white up to halfway through. Grind some more cracked pepper onto the exposed uncooked surface before flipping over and cooking through. Grill or sauté the mangoes and serve with the fish.

Salmon Delight

SERVES 4

A recipe from the radiant Katrina Price.

4 skinless salmon steaks

4 slices prosciutto

12 cherry tomatoes

8 ounces green beans

Preheat the oven to 350°F. Wrap the salmon steaks in prosciutto and place in a baking dish. Add the cherry tomatoes and beans. Bake for 10 to 15 minutes.

OPTIONAL: For a special occasion, top with some toasted pine nuts and a drizzle of lemon juice.

Salmon Roulade

SERVES 4

Recipe by Chef Dan Primmer.

4 salmon steaks (8 ounces each)

7 ounces feta, crumbled

7 ounces semi-dried tomatoes, chopped

3 ounces baby spinach

Preheat the oven to 350°F. Cut a 16-inch-long piece of foil and lay it flat. Place the same length of parchment paper on top. Butterfly each salmon steak (cut in half lengthwise without cutting all the way through) and place the steaks in the middle of the foil side by side, touching. In a bowl, combine the remaining ingredients and spread the mixture on the salmon. Use the foil and paper to roll the salmon into a tight roll, twisting the ends to secure the contents. Place on a baking sheet and bake for 15 to 20 minutes. Slice to serve.

OPTIONAL: Serve with Butter Bean & Potato Puree (page 85) or Arugula & Parmesan Salad (page 75).

Salmon with Honey & Mint

SERVES 4

1 tablespoon honey

1 tablespoon chopped fresh mint

1 lime, ½ juiced and ½ sliced

4 salmon steaks

In a shallow dish, combine the honey, mint, lime juice, and sea salt and pepper to taste. Add the salmon and marinate for 10 to 15 minutes. Preheat the broiler to high. Lift the salmon from the marinade, allowing the excess to drip off. Broil for 5 to 8 minutes, depending on the thickness of the salmon. Serve garnished with the lime slices.

Snapper with Almond Crust

SERVES 4

A recipe from Michelle Dodd to delight even the fussiest fish eaters.

2 ounces Parmesan cheese, finely grated

1 cup almond meal

2 eggs

4 medium snapper fillets

Preheat the oven to 425°F. Line a baking sheet with parchment paper. In a shallow medium bowl, combine the Parmesan and almond meal. Beat the eggs in a second shallow bowl. Dip the fish fillets, one at a time, into the egg and then into the almond mixture to coat both sides. Place the fish in a single layer on the baking sheet. Bake for 20 minutes, or until cooked to your liking.

NOTE: Cut into small fingers for "fish fingers with a twist" that kids will love!

Sunshine Shrimp

SERVES 4

A recipe from Dan Primmer. One word—FABALICIOUS! Delicious served over steamed rice.

1 can (14 ounces) coconut cream

20 shrimp, peeled and deveined

½ fresh pineapple, diced

2 large mild red chile peppers, chopped

In a nonstick skillet, bring the coconut cream to a boil over medium heat. Reduce the heat, add the remaining ingredients, and simmer until warmed through and the shrimp turn orange.

Swiss Fish

SERVES 4

2 tablespoons butter

4 white fish fillets

4 slices Swiss cheese

1 avocado, thinly sliced

Preheat the oven to 350°F. Line a baking sheet with parchment paper. In a nonstick skillet, melt the butter over medium heat. Add the fish fillets and cook for about 2 minutes before flipping (time will depend on how thick the fish fillets are). Place the cooked fillets on the baking sheet and top with the Swiss cheese. Bake for 5 minutes to melt the cheese and serve topped with the sliced avocado.

Tandoori Salmon

SERVES 4

*Serve over a bed of salad with cilantro,
drizzled with lime juice.*

- 2 tablespoons olive oil
- 4 salmon fillets
- 2 tablespoons GF tandoori paste
- ⅓ cup plain yogurt

Preheat the oven to 400°F. Line a baking sheet with parchment paper. Rub half the oil over the salmon fillets and season with sea salt to taste. Brush with the tandoori paste. In a large nonstick skillet, heat the remaining oil over high heat. Add the salmon, skin side down, and cook for 2 minutes. Flip and cook until golden. Transfer to the baking sheet and bake for 8 minutes for medium, or until cooked to your liking. Serve with a dollop of yogurt.

Tuna & Tomato Risotto

SERVES 4

A recipe from the talented Marie McColl.

- 5 cups GF vegetable stock
- 2 cups Arborio rice
- 3 cans (5 ounces each) water-packed tuna, drained and flaked
- 1 can (14.5 ounces) chopped tomatoes

In a saucepan, bring the stock to a boil. Add the rice, reduce the heat, and simmer for 20 minutes. Add the tuna, tomatoes, and sea salt and pepper to taste. Continue to simmer, stirring often, until all the liquid has been absorbed.

LAMB

From what we get, we can make a living; what we give, however, makes a life.
—Arthur Ashe

Bocconcini Lamb Chops

SERVES 4

4 loin lamb chops

4 pieces roasted red pepper

2 tablespoons lemon juice

6 bocconcini (small balls of mozzarella), sliced

Preheat the broiler. In a nonstick skillet, cook the lamb until lightly browned. Put the chops on a nonstick baking sheet. Combine the pepper pieces and lemon juice in a small bowl. Top the chops with the peppers and bocconcini. Season to taste with sea salt and pepper. Broil for about 5 minutes, or until the cheese melts and the topping is nice and warm.

Chinese-Style Lamb Roast

SERVES 4 TO 6

Try it . . . You'll be surprised! Serve with fried rice.

3½-pound leg of lamb, tied

¾ cup evaporated milk

¼ cup GF hoisin or GF teriyaki sauce

Preheat the oven to 350°F. Place the lamb in a large oven bag. Combine the milk and sauce. Pour over the lamb and tightly seal the bag, piercing a few holes around the end. Place the lamb in a roasting pan and roast for 1 hour and 45 minutes, or until cooked as desired. Thickly slice the roast across the grain.

OPTIONAL: Garnish with cilantro.

Glazed Lamb Chops

SERVES 4 TO 6

4 to 6 loin lamb chops (¾ inch thick)

½ to ¾ cup orange marmalade

2 tablespoons lemon juice

Preheat the broiler. Broil the lamb for 6 minutes. Season with sea salt and pepper, flip, and grill for 5 minutes, or until almost cooked. Season the second side. Combine the marmalade and lemon juice and spread evenly over the lamb. Grill for 2 minutes longer.

Lamb Chops with Roast Pepper Mayonnaise

SERVES 4

1 cup roasted red peppers

½ cup GF mayonnaise

8 mid-loin lamb chops

In a mini chopper, puree the peppers and mayonnaise until smooth. Preheat a nonstick grill pan. Put in the lamb and cook to the desired doneness. Serve the chops with a dollop of pepper mayonnaise.

Lamb Cutlets Kilpatrick

SERVES 4

These are really scrummy! Morgan is ten and asks for these every week!!!

16 rib lamb chops

½ cup GF barbecue sauce

6 slices bacon, chopped and lightly fried

Preheat the broiler. Broil the chops until just cooked through. Spread the barbecue sauce evenly over each chop. Sprinkle with the bacon and return to the broiler for a few minutes to crisp up the bacon.

Lamb Pesto Cutlets

SERVES 4

Everyone looooooooooooooves these!

16 rib lamb chops

¼ cup GF basil pesto

¼ cup grated Parmesan cheese

Preheat the broiler. Line a baking sheet with parchment paper. Place the chops on the baking sheet and broil until cooked through. Combine the pesto and Parmesan. Spread the chops with the pesto mixture and return to the broiler to get the topping golden and crusty.

Lamb, Rosemary & Chorizo Skewers

MAKES 6 KEBABS

Delicious!

4 loin lamb chops, meat cut into 24 pieces

2 GF cured chorizo sausages, cut into 24 thick slices

4 sprigs fresh rosemary

⅓ cup olive oil

Combine all the ingredients in a bowl and let marinate for 30 minutes. Preheat the oven to 400°F. Line a baking sheet with parchment paper. On each of 6 skewers, thread 2 pieces of lamb and 2 slices of chorizo, alternating them. Place the skewers on the baking sheet, drizzle with any remaining rosemary oil, and bake for 10 minutes, or until done to your liking.

Roast Lamb

SERVES 4 TO 6

A recipe by the lovely Jan Neale.
Serve with roast vegetables and GF gravy.

2¼ pounds leg of lamb or lamb shoulder

2 cloves garlic, sliced

Leaves from 2 sprigs rosemary

1 tablespoon olive oil

Preheat the oven to 400°F. Cut 6 slits 1 inch deep and 1 inch long in the lamb. Press a slice of garlic into each slit. Place the lamb in a large roasting pan. Sprinkle with the rosemary and drizzle with the oil. Season with sea salt and pepper to taste. Roast for 1 hour, or until cooked to your liking.

Tangy Lamb Balls

SERVES 4

A fabulous recipe that is definitely worth trying,
from Perditta O'Connor. Serve with jasmine rice.

1 pound ground lamb

1 teaspoon GF curry powder

3 tablespoons GF Thai sweet chili sauce

Juice of 1 lemon

In a large bowl, combine all the ingredients. Form into balls. Preheat a nonstick skillet. Put in the lamb and cook until crunchy on the outside (this means it is cooked well on the inside).

OPTIONAL: Add a clove of garlic to the mixture and serve with a mint-yogurt dipping sauce.

NOTE: These also make a good appetizer. Roll into small balls and serve with additional GF Thai sweet chili sauce.

Teriyaki Lamb Skewers

SERVES 4

2 tablespoons GF soy sauce

2 tablespoons mirin

1 teaspoon superfine sugar

1⅓ pounds lamb, cut into cubes

In a bowl, combine all the ingredients. Let sit about 30 minutes for the flavors to develop. Thread the lamb on bamboo skewers that have been soaking in cold water. Cook under the broiler or on the grill for 3 to 4 minutes on each side for medium, or until done to your liking.

PASTA

What we learned when cooking with gluten-free pasta is that you need to follow the manufacturer's instructions! Overcooking gluten-free pasta results in thick, gluggy pasta that your guests will tease you about all night!!!!

Alfredo
SERVES 4

This is simply sensational!

1 pound GF fettuccine

4 tablespoons (½ stick) butter

1 cup heavy cream

4 ounces Parmesan cheese, shaved

Cook the pasta according to package directions. Drain. Meanwhile, in a large saucepan, melt the butter, add the cream, and bring to a boil. Simmer for 5 minutes, stirring constantly. Add three-fourths of the Parmesan and season well. Reduce the heat, add the drained pasta, and toss until thoroughly coated. Serve sprinkled with the remaining Parmesan.

Beef & Butternut Squash Pasta
SERVES 4

1 pound extra-lean ground beef

2 cups GF pasta sauce

12 ounces butternut squash, peeled and cubed

1 pound GF spiral pasta

In a large nonstick skillet, brown the beef. Add the pasta sauce and bring to a boil. Reduce the heat and simmer for 20 minutes. In a steamer, cook the squash until tender, then fold into the beef mixture. Meanwhile, cook the pasta according to package directions. Drain and serve topped with the beef and butternut squash sauce.

Blue Broccoli Penne Pasta

SERVES 4

1 pound GF penne pasta

1 large head broccoli, cut into florets

4 ounces blue cheese

1 cup sour cream

Cook the pasta according to package directions. Drain. Meanwhile, cook the broccoli in a saucepan of boiling water for 4 minutes, or until just cooked through. Drain. In a nonstick skillet, cook the blue cheese and sour cream over low heat until reduced to a thick, creamy sauce. Toss with the broccoli and pasta, heat through, and serve warm.

OPTIONAL: Serve topped with toasted pine nuts.

Florentine Carbonara

SERVES 4

Recipe from Julie Stephens. This is timeless!

1 pound GF spaghetti

5 slices bacon, diced

2 eggs, lightly beaten

4 ounces Parmesan cheese, shaved

Cook the pasta according to package directions. Meanwhile, in a nonstick skillet, cook the bacon. Drain the pasta and add the eggs immediately, stirring to coat the hot pasta. Add the bacon and Parmesan and toss to combine. Serve immediately.

OPTIONAL: Cook the bacon with a little garlic.

Gnocchi

MAKES ABOUT 30

This is fabulous!

1½ cups GF all-purpose flour

1 cup ricotta cheese

1 egg yolk

Sift the flour into a bowl. Add the ricotta and egg yolk and, with your hands, mix into a smooth dough. (If the mixture is too sticky, add a little more flour.) Roll into ¾-inch balls. With a fork, press down on a ball and pull it toward yourself. As you work, set the gnocchi aside, covered to prevent drying. Bring a pot of salted water to a boil. Add the gnocchi and when they float, they're done.

OPTIONAL: Panfry the gnocchi in butter until light golden brown.

Gnocchi with Buttery Thyme Sauce

SERVES 4

8 tablespoons (1 stick) butter

1 tablespoon fresh thyme leaves

1 pound GF gnocchi

⅓ cup shaved Pecorino Romano cheese

In a heavy skillet over medium heat, cook the butter for 2 minutes, or until it just begins to brown. Remove from the heat and add the thyme leaves. Cook the gnocchi in a large pot of boiling salted water until they rise to the surface, about 4 minutes. Using a slotted spoon, transfer the gnocchi to the hot butter sauce and toss to coat. Spoon into shallow bowls, season with sea salt and pepper to taste, and top with the Pecorino Romano before serving.

Homemade Napolitana Sauce

SERVES 4

2 tablespoons olive oil

2 cloves garlic, crushed through a press

1 can (14.5 ounces) diced tomatoes

Leaves from ½ bunch basil

In a nonstick skillet, heat the oil over medium heat. Add the garlic and cook, stirring, for 30 seconds. Add the tomatoes and sea salt and pepper to taste. Simmer over low heat for 10 minutes. Stir in the basil and simmer for 5 minutes.

Macaroni Bake

SERVES 4

A recipe from the wonderful Jenny Postle.

4 cups cooked GF macaroni

1 can (10.75 ounces) GF condensed tomato soup

8 ounces GF ham or bacon, diced

4 ounces grated Cheddar cheese

Preheat the oven to 350°F. In a bowl, combine the macaroni, tomato soup, ham or bacon, and half the Cheddar. Mix well and transfer to a baking dish. Top with the remaining cheese and bake for 20 minutes.

OPTIONAL: Mix some freshly grated GF bread crumbs into the cheese topping.

Pasta with Tomato & Basil

SERVES 4

The kids will love this, too.

1 pound GF pasta

2 cups GF pasta sauce with herbs

2 ounces Parmesan cheese, shaved

Leaves from ½ bunch basil, torn (see Note); a few whole leaves reserved for garnish

Cook the pasta until not quite al dente. Drain. In a large saucepan, heat the pasta sauce. Add the drained pasta to the simmering sauce along with most of the Parmesan. When the pasta is al dente, stir in the basil leaves. Serve with the remaining Parmesan and garnish with a few basil leaves.

NOTE: Basil leaves are best torn rather than chopped, as they don't bruise when torn.

Pesto Fettuccine

SERVES 4

This is so flavorsome!

8 ounces GF fettuccine

1 cup heavy cream

½ cup GF basil pesto

¼ cup chopped chives, plus extra for garnish

Cook the pasta according to package directions. Drain, reserving ¼ cup of the cooking liquid. Return the pasta to the pan. In a medium skillet, combine the cream and pesto. Cook, stirring, over low heat for 5 minutes, or until the mixture comes to a boil. Add the cream mixture, the reserved cooking liquid, and the ¼ cup chives to the pasta and toss gently. Season with sea salt and pepper to taste and toss again. Serve garnished with the extra chives.

Pesto Pasta

SERVES 4

1 pound GF fettuccine

1¼ cups GF basil pesto

6 ounces cherry tomatoes, halved

4 ounces Parmesan cheese, grated

Cook the pasta according to package directions. Drain and return to the pot. Stir in the pesto, tossing gently over low heat until the pasta is coated. Add the tomatoes and toss for 1 minute. Serve sprinkled with the Parmesan.

Pine Nut Pasta

SERVES 2

2 tablespoons butter

½ cup pine nuts (about 2½ ounces)

8 ounces GF fettuccine

2 ounces Parmesan cheese, grated

In a nonstick skillet, melt the butter. Add the pine nuts and cook until golden brown. Cook the pasta according to package directions. Drain and return to the pot. Toss with the pine nuts and Parmesan.

OPTIONAL: A little cracked pepper tastes great, too.

Sun-Dried Pesto Pasta

SERVES 4

*A recipe by Alistair Beattie that surprised us
with its simplicity and taste!*

1 pound GF spaghetti

4 slices bacon, diced

¼ cup GF sun-dried
tomato pesto

⅓ cup pine nuts (about
3 ounces), toasted (see
Note)

Cook the pasta according to package directions. Meanwhile, in a skillet, brown the bacon. When the pasta is ready, drain, rinse with boiling water, and return to the pot. Toss with the pesto, bacon, and pine nuts. Add more pesto, if desired.

NOTE: Toast the pine nuts for 2 to 3 minutes in a preheated 350°F oven.

PORK

Bacon & Cannellini Risotto

SERVES 4

S.c.r.u.m.p.t.i.o.u.s!

4 slices bacon, coarsely chopped

5 cups GF chicken stock

2 cups Arborio rice

1 can (15 ounces) cannellini beans

In a large nonstick skillet, cook the bacon until crisp. In a saucepan, bring the stock to a boil. Add the rice to the skillet and stir well. Add the stock, reduce the heat, cover, and simmer for 20 minutes. Add the beans and sea salt and pepper to taste. Simmer until the rice is tender and the stock has been fully absorbed.

OPTIONAL: Replace the cannellini beans with peas.

Country BBQ Pork Ribs

SERVES 6

4½ pounds pork ribs

2 large onions, sliced

1 clove garlic, crushed through a press

1½ cups of your favorite GF barbecue sauce

Place the ribs in a slow cooker. Add the onions, garlic, and barbecue sauce. Cover and cook on low for 7 to 8 hours.

Dill & Honey Pork Chops

SERVES 6

1 tablespoon olive oil

6 thick pork chops

2 tablespoons honey

1 teaspoon snipped fresh dill

In a nonstick skillet, heat the oil over medium-high heat. Panfry the chops for 3 minutes on each side, then remove from the heat. In a bowl, combine the honey and dill and coat each chop. Return the chops to the pan and cook for 1 minute, turning once. Scrape the remaining glaze over the chops after turning.

Paprika Chops

SERVES 2

1½ teaspoons paprika

1½ teaspoons white pepper

2 large pork chops

2 tablespoons olive oil

Preheat the oven to 400°F. Mix together the paprika, white pepper, and a pinch of sea salt. Coat the chops lightly with olive oil. Rub the spice mixture evenly over the pork with your fingers. Place the chops on a baking sheet and bake for 15 to 25 minutes, or until the juices run clear.

Pork & Coconut Satay Sticks

SERVES 4

In the words of Michelle Dodd, "These are the best!"

Scant 1 cup coconut milk

2 tablespoons crunchy peanut butter

2 teaspoons GF curry powder

1 pound pork, cut for stir-fry

Mix together the coconut milk, peanut butter, curry powder, and sea salt and pepper to taste until smooth and blended. Add the pork and marinate in the fridge overnight. Soak 12 bamboo skewers in water. Preheat the grill to high. Thread the pork on the skewers and grill, turning constantly so as not to burn. Continue to glaze with the marinade while cooking.

Pork & Winter Squash Curry

SERVES 4

1 pound pork, cubed

2 tablespoons GF Thai red curry paste

1 can (14 ounces) coconut cream

1 pound winter squash cubes

In a large saucepan, brown the pork over medium heat. Add the curry paste and cook, stirring, for 5 minutes. Add the coconut cream, ½ cup water, the squash, and sea salt and pepper to taste. Bring to a boil, then reduce to a simmer and cook for 30 minutes, or until the pork is cooked.

NOTE: This is best made a few hours prior to serving, as it thickens while cooling. Simply reheat when ready to serve.

Pork Roll

SERVES 4

Serve with either apple or tomato sauce . . .
Surprisingly yummy!

1 pound GF pork sausages, casings removed

1 egg

1 onion, grated

1 cup fresh GF bread crumbs, toasted

Preheat the oven to 350°F. Mix together the sausage meat, egg, onion, and sea salt and pepper to taste. Form into a loaf and roll in the bread crumbs. Place in a baking dish and bake for 20 minutes. Flip over and cook for 20 minutes longer.

Pork with Parmesan Polenta

SERVES 2

Recipe by the talented Matt Tebbutt.

4 pork chops (see Note)

4 cups GF vegetable stock

1 cup polenta

¾ cup finely grated
Parmesan cheese

Preheat the oven to 375°F. Preheat a skillet. Put the pork chops in the skillet, season with sea salt, and cook for 2 to 3 minutes (depending on thickness) before turning. Cook for 2 to 3 minutes on the second side, or until the juices run clear. Transfer to a rimmed baking sheet and bake for 5 minutes. Meanwhile, in a saucepan, bring 3 cups of the stock to a boil. Add the polenta. It should not thicken too much but should be very creamy (add more stock if necessary). Add the Parmesan and season with sea salt and pepper to taste. Spoon the polenta onto 2 plates and place 2 chops on top of it. Pour any juices from the baking sheet on top.

NOTE: If the chops are quite large, this may make 3 or 4 servings.

Pork with Vermicelli

SERVES 2

10 ounces ground pork

½ cup GF oyster sauce

2 scallions, cut into ¾-inch strips

4 ounces GF bean vermicelli

Combine the pork, oyster sauce, and scallions. Refrigerate for about 1 hour. Soak the vermicelli in warm water for 5 to 10 minutes, or until soft. Drain. Preheat a nonstick skillet. Add the marinated pork and stir-fry, breaking it up with a spatula, until browned. Add the vermicelli and stir-fry quickly until the noodles are heated. Serve immediately.

Rich Tomato Pork

SERVES 4

A recipe from the lovely Tanya Ormsby.

4 pork chops

2 cloves garlic, crushed through a press

1 can (14.5 ounces) diced tomatoes with basil and garlic or oregano and basil

½ cup heavy cream

Preheat a nonstick skillet. Put in the pork chops and cook until golden on both sides. Add the garlic and tomatoes, bring to a boil, then reduce to a simmer and cook for 15 minutes (you may need a little more tomato mixture, depending on the size of the chops). Just before serving, add the cream and increase the heat to thicken the sauce.

SERVE with Mashed Potatoes (page 89) and Green Beans & Pine Nuts (page 95).

Sausage Snacks

SERVES 4

A recipe from Errol McCosker.

4 large GF pork sausages

¼ cup GF sweet mustard pickle

2 tablespoons finely chopped chives or parsley (optional)

2 cups mashed potatoes

Broil or fry the sausages. Let cool slightly; then split open lengthwise. Spread with the pickle. Stir the chives or parsley (if using) into the mashed potatoes and spoon onto the sausages. Place under the broiler and cook until the potatoes are golden brown.

OPTIONAL: GF ketchup can be substituted for GF sweet mustard pickle.

Sausages with Caramelized Onions

SERVES 2

4 GF sausages

1 onion, sliced

¼ cup packed light brown sugar

1 tomato, finely diced

Preheat a grill pan. Grill the sausages until cooked through. Set aside to cool slightly. Put the onion slices into the fat remaining in the pan and grill until browned. Sprinkle with the brown sugar and cook until caramelized. To serve, score the sausages lengthwise with a sharp knife, fill with the onion, and top with the diced tomato.

Spareribs

SERVES 6 TO 8

4½ pounds pork spareribs

Generous ¾ cup GF barbecue sauce

Juice of 1 orange

Put the ribs in a large pot with water to cover. Simmer for 1 hour. Drain. Preheat the oven to 350°F. Line a rimmed baking sheet with parchment paper. Mix together the barbecue sauce and 1 cup juice and pour over the ribs. Bake for 30 to 40 minutes, basting every 10 minutes, until done to your liking.

Tangy Pork Chops

SERVES 4

4 pork chops

½ cup honey

¼ cup GF Worcestershire sauce

¼ cup GF ketchup

Preheat the broiler. Broil the chops until lightly browned. Turn the oven to 350°F. Transfer the chops to a shallow baking dish. Combine the remaining ingredients and pour over the chops. Cover and bake for 45 minutes.

Asparagus Omelet

SERVES 4

Recipe by Janelle McCosker.

2 tablespoons butter

16 asparagus spears, cut into ¾-inch pieces

8 eggs

1 teaspoon paprika

In a medium skillet, melt the butter over medium heat. Add the asparagus and cook until heated through. In a bowl, beat the eggs and season with sea salt and pepper to taste. Preheat a nonstick skillet and pour in the eggs. Sprinkle the asparagus over the eggs and cook over medium heat until the eggs are set. Serve sprinkled with paprika.

OPTIONAL FILLINGS: Classic: GF ham, tomato, mushroom, onion, and cheese. Middle Eastern: crumbled goat cheese and arugula. Asian: crabmeat, cilantro, and GF oyster sauce. Mediterranean: feta, olives, and sun-dried tomatoes.

Baked Ricotta & Thyme Pie

SERVES 6 TO 8

This is super yummy served with a salad and delicious dressing!

1 container (32 ounces) ricotta cheese

3 eggs, lightly beaten

½ bunch fresh thyme

Preheat the oven to 400°F. Line an 8-inch springform pan with parchment paper. In a bowl, stir together the ricotta and eggs. Scrape the mixture into the pan and sprinkle generously with thyme. Season with sea salt and pepper to taste. Bake for 35 to 40 minutes, or until firm and golden. Let cool before removing the rim from the pan. Let rest for 10 minutes, then cut into wedges and serve.

OPTIONAL: This recipe can also be made in muffin tins. Reduce the baking time to 15 minutes, or until the pies are firm and golden. They are lovely served with a crisp garden salad.

Broccoli & Lemon Risotto

SERVES 2

1 bunch broccoli

1 cup Arborio rice

1 lemon

2 ounces Parmesan cheese, grated

Cut the broccoli florets off the stalk. Then cut the stalks into matchsticks. In a steamer, cook the florets until barely tender. In a skillet, cook the broccoli stalks in ¼ cup water until just tender, then drain. In a saucepan, bring 4¼ cups salted water to a boil. Add the rice and cook, stirring regularly, until all the liquid is absorbed. Grate the zest of the lemon into the rice, then add the juice of the lemon and half of the Parmesan, stirring to mix. Add the broccoli and mix gently. Season with sea salt and pepper to taste. Serve with the remaining Parmesan.

Cheddar & Basil Tortillas

SERVES 1

1 tablespoon butter

2 GF tortillas (8-inch)

2 ounces Cheddar cheese, grated

Leaves from ¼ bunch basil

In a nonstick skillet, heat the butter over medium heat. Add one tortilla, sprinkle with the Cheddar and basil, and season with sea salt and pepper to taste. Cook for 2 minutes, or until golden brown on the bottom. Top with the remaining tortilla and flip. Cook for 2 to 3 minutes longer. Slide from the pan onto a cutting board and cut into wedges. Serve immediately.

OPTIONAL: Swap out the basil for sun-dried tomatoes, mushrooms, GF relish, or whatever you like.

Eggplant & Ricotta Pasta

SERVES 4

Y.U.M.M.Y!

1 pound GF penne pasta

1 cup GF marinated eggplant

2 cups GF tomato and basil pasta sauce

8 ounces ricotta cheese

Cook the pasta according to package directions. Drain. Meanwhile, in a saucepan, combine the eggplant and the sauce and simmer for 10 minutes, until warm. Divide the pasta among 4 bowls and top with the sauce and ricotta.

Eggplant & Sweet Potato Curry

SERVES 4

This is really delicious! Serve with rice and pita bread.

2 onions, sliced

1 eggplant, cut into ¾-inch cubes

1 sweet potato (6 ounces), peeled and cut into large chunks

1 jar (12 ounces) GF korma curry sauce

In a nonstick skillet, simmer the onions in a little water for just 1 minute. Drain and set aside. In the same skillet, cook the eggplant until evenly browned. Add the onions and sweet potato. Empty the jar of korma sauce into the skillet, then fill the empty jar halfway with water and add to the pan. Simmer for 20 to 30 minutes, or until the sweet potato and eggplant are tender.

Eggplant Parmigiana

SERVES 4

1 medium eggplant

2 tablespoons butter

1 cup GF marinara sauce

¾ cup grated Parmesan cheese

Slice the eggplant into 6 pieces about 1 to 1½ inches thick. Lightly season each slice with sea salt and pepper. In a nonstick skillet over medium heat, melt the butter and sauté the eggplant slices for 2 minutes on each side, or until lightly browned. Remove to a baking sheet and top each slice with the marinara sauce and Parmesan. Place under the broiler for 2 minutes, or until the cheese melts.

OPTIONAL: Sprinkle with freshly torn basil and serve with a crisp garden salad.

Frittata

SERVES 4

A recipe by Katrina Price.

6 eggs

1 small bunch spinach, chopped

4 ounces Parmesan cheese, grated

½ cup GF bread crumbs

Preheat the oven to 300°F. Beat the eggs with a whisk until light and fluffy. Add the spinach, Parmesan, and bread crumbs. Season with sea salt and pepper to taste. Line a 9-inch quiche pan with parchment paper. Pour in the mixture and bake for 20 minutes.

OPTIONAL: Add cinnamon if desired. (Oprah says it's good for the brain, so we are using it to season everything!!!)

Mushroom & Garlic Pizza

MAKES 2

Recipe from Rodger Fishwick.

2 GF tortillas (8-inch)

2 teaspoons minced garlic

4 ounces button mushrooms, sliced

2 ounces mozzarella cheese, shredded

Preheat the oven to 350°F. Line a baking sheet with parchment paper. Arrange the tortillas on the baking sheet. Spread with the garlic and top with the mushrooms. Sprinkle the mozzarella on top. Bake for 10 minutes.

Nachos

SERVES 2

Recipe from Trudy Graham.

1 package (3 ounces) GF corn chips

½ cup GF salsa

3 ounces Cheddar cheese, grated

½ avocado, mashed

Layer the corn chips in a microwaveable dish. Top with the salsa and Cheddar. Microwave until the cheese melts. Serve topped with the avocado.

OPTIONAL: Add some refried beans, diced tomato, or sour cream. Broil instead of microwaving.

Nachos with Chiles & Olives

SERVES 4

4 ounces GF tortilla chips

6 tablespoons sliced pickled jalapeño chiles

4 ounces black olives, pitted and sliced

½ pound Cheddar cheese, grated

Preheat the oven to 350°F. Lay the tortilla chips in a large ovenproof dish. Sprinkle with the jalapeños, olives, and Cheddar and bake for 12 to 15 minutes, or until the cheese is melted and bubbling.

OPTIONAL: Serve with your favorite salsa for dipping.

Polenta Cakes

SERVES 4

Inspired by Naomi Carter.

3 cups GF vegetable stock

1 cup polenta

4 ounces Parmesan cheese, grated

3 tablespoons butter

Grease an 8-inch round cake pan. In a saucepan, bring the stock to a boil and stir in the polenta. Continue stirring until the mixture has thickened and is creamy. Add the Parmesan and butter and mix well. Season with sea salt and pepper to taste. Spoon the polenta into the cake pan and refrigerate until completely cold. Cut into 8 wedges. Preheat a nonstick skillet. Put in the polenta cakes and cook until crisp and golden on both sides.

OPTIONAL: For a little green, add some peas.

Spanish Tortilla

SERVES 4

¼ cup olive oil

2 potatoes, peeled and thinly sliced

1 medium onion, diced

8 eggs

In a nonstick skillet, heat the oil over medium heat. Add the potatoes and onion and cook for 2 to 3 minutes. Whisk the eggs and season with sea salt and pepper to taste. Pour the eggs over the potatoes and onion and cook for 10 minutes. Run under the broiler for 2 minutes to brown. Let cool before cutting into wedges to serve.

OPTIONAL: Scallions can replace the onion. Pepper strips sautéed in oil, small bits of chorizo, cooked bacon or shrimp, or strips of prosciutto can be stirred into the eggs, too!

NOTE: To keep eggs fresh, store in the fridge in their carton as soon as possible after purchase. An egg will age more in a day at room temperature than it will in a week in the fridge.

Spinach Pie

SERVES 2

A recipe from Karyn Turnbull-Markus.

1 small bunch spinach, chopped

8 ounces cottage cheese

1 clove garlic, crushed through a press

2 eggs, lightly beaten

Preheat the oven to 350°F. In a medium saucepan of boiling water, cook the spinach for 5 minutes. Drain and gently squeeze dry. In a small baking dish, layer the spinach, cottage cheese, and garlic. As you work, spoon a little beaten egg over each layer. Continue until all the ingredients are used, ending with the cottage cheese. Season with cracked black pepper. Bake for 20 minutes, or until the pie is slightly brown on top.

Yam & Feta Frittata

SERVES 4

*A fabulous dinner for anyone. This is delicious served
with a crisp green salad.*

2¼ pounds yams, peeled and cut into ½-inch slices

2 tablespoons olive oil

8 ounces feta cheese, crumbled

6 eggs

Preheat the oven to 400°F. Spread the yams on a baking sheet and sprinkle with 1 tablespoon of the oil. Bake for 20 minutes, or until tender. Turn the oven to broil. In a nonstick skillet, heat the remaining 1 tablespoon oil over medium heat. Add the yams and feta. Whisk the eggs and season with sea salt and pepper to taste. Pour the eggs into the skillet. Reduce the heat to low and cook for 5 minutes, or until the base is set. Place the frittata under the broiler and broil for 7 minutes, or until cooked through. Let cool slightly, then cut into wedges.

DESSERTS

"It's not you, it's the dress!"

—Beth from Bondi Markets, Sydney

Almond Slices

MAKES 15 SLICES

Recipe from Cyndi O'Meara.

4 egg whites

½ cup sugar

1 cup GF all-purpose flour

5 ounces sliced almonds

Preheat the oven to 350°F. Grease a 9 by 5 by 3-inch loaf pan or line with parchment paper. With an electric mixer, beat the egg whites until stiff peaks form. Add the sugar and beat for 1 minute. Stir in the flour and almonds. Scrape the batter into the loaf pan and bake for 40 minutes. (Leave the oven on.) Turn the loaf out to cool slightly, then slice thinly. Place the slices on a baking sheet and return to the oven for 10 to 15 minutes, or until browned.

Apple Bars

SERVES 8

A recipe from the lovely Trudy Graham. This is dynamite!

1 box GF golden butter cake mix

8 tablespoons (1 stick) butter, melted

1 can (22 ounces) no-sugar-added apple pie filling

¾ cup plus 2 tablespoons sour cream

Preheat the oven to 350°F. Line a 13 by 9-inch baking dish with parchment paper. Combine the cake mix and butter and press into the baking dish. Bake for 15 minutes. Meanwhile, in a bowl, mix the apple pie filling and sour cream. Remove the base from the oven and top with the apple mix. Return to the oven for 15 minutes. Let cool completely and then refrigerate before cutting into bars.

OPTIONAL: Add 1 cup shredded coconut to the base mix. Sprinkle the apple mix with cinnamon before baking.

Apple Crumble

SERVES 4 TO 6

Serve with cream or ice cream.

1 can (22 ounces) no-sugar-added apple pie filling

¾ cup packed light brown sugar

1 cup GF all-purpose flour

8 tablespoons (1 stick) butter, at room temperature

Preheat the oven to 400°F. Spread the apple pie the filling in a 9-inch square baking dish. Sprinkle with 2 tablespoons of the brown sugar. In a bowl, combine the flour and remaining brown sugar. Add 6 tablespoons of the butter and blend in until crumbly. Sprinkle on top of the apple filling. Melt the remaining 2 tablespoons butter and drizzle on top. Bake for 30 minutes, or until golden brown.

OPTIONAL: Add ½ teaspoon pumpkin pie spice to the apple mix.

Baked Rice Custard

SERVES 4

This is really easy and really tasty!

1 cup rice

1 can (14 ounces) condensed milk

3 eggs, lightly beaten

¼ cup raisins

Preheat the oven to 350°F. In a large pan of boiling water, cook the rice for 10 minutes. Drain. In a bowl, combine the rice, the condensed milk, 1¾ cups water, the eggs, and raisins. Pour into a shallow 10 by 14-inch baking dish. Place the dish in a larger pan and pour into the large pan enough hot water to come halfway up the sides of the dish. Bake for 40 minutes, or until set.

OPTIONAL: Sprinkle with nutmeg before baking.

Baked Ricotta with Blueberry Sauce

SERVES 4

Kim's favorite! Dish this up to the applause of all!

2 egg whites

6 tablespoons honey

8 ounces ricotta cheese

2 cups frozen blueberries, thawed

Preheat the oven to 350°F. Line a 9-inch round cake pan with parchment paper. With an electric mixer, beat the egg whites until stiff peaks form. In a bowl, stir together 4 tablespoons of the honey and all the ricotta. Fold in the egg whites. Spread the mixture in the pan and bake for 40 minutes, or until it rises and is golden. Meanwhile, gently heat the berries in a small saucepan until softened. Stir in the remaining 2 tablespoons honey and simmer for 20 minutes. Serve the blueberry sauce over the ricotta pie wedges.

Blue Chockie Mousse

SERVES 4

This is berry, berry nice!

8 ounces blueberries

8 ounces dark chocolate

1¼ cups heavy cream

Divide the blueberries among 4 small ramekins. In a microwaveable bowl, melt the chocolate in 15-second increments, stirring after each. Remove and let cool. Beat the cream until soft peaks form, then fold into the melted chocolate. Spoon the mixture over the blueberries and serve immediately.

Cheesecake Crust

MAKES 1 REALLY DELICIOUS CRUST

6 ounces GF cookies (vanilla wafer imitation)

½ cup almond meal

5 tablespoons butter, melted

In a blender or food processor, process the cookies to fine crumbs. Transfer to a bowl. Add the almond meal and melted butter and mix thoroughly. Pat into the bottom of a greased or parchment paper–lined springform pan or pie plate and chill before using.

Cheesecake Filling #1

8 ounces cream cheese, at room temperature

6 ounces vanilla yogurt

4 egg yolks

2 cups mixed fresh or thawed frozen berries

Preheat the oven to 350°F. In a bowl, mix together the cream cheese, yogurt, and egg yolks until smooth. Fold in the berries. Pour into a GF crust (see above) and bake for 50 minutes.

OPTIONAL: Serve with Raspberry Sauce (page 21).

Cheesecake Filling #2

8 ounces cream cheese, at room temperature

1 can (14 ounces) condensed milk

1 envelope (0.25 ounce) unflavored gelatin

In a medium bowl, beat the cream cheese until smooth. Add the condensed milk and beat until thick and creamy. Mix the gelatin into 3 tablespoons warm water, stirring vigorously until dissolved. Add to the bowl and mix thoroughly for 3 minutes to make sure the gelatin is evenly distributed through the mixture. Pour into a GF crust (see page 172) and chill for 2 to 3 hours, allowing time for the mixture to set, before serving.

OPTIONAL: This is pretty served topped with freshly sliced strawberries and kiwifruits.

Chocolate & Coconut Clusters
MAKES 24

Recipe from Shirley Bermingham.

5 ounces dark chocolate

3½ cups GF cornflakes

10 tablespoons shredded coconut

½ cup raisins

Line a 24-cup mini muffin tin with paper liners. In a microwaveable medium bowl, melt the dark chocolate in 15-second increments, stirring well after each. Add the cornflakes and coconut to the chocolate and stir well. Spoon into the muffin cups. Top with the raisins. Refrigerate for at least 1 hour to set.

Chocolate-Dipped Lychees

MAKES ABOUT 12

A recipe from Meg Wilson. These are elegant, easy, and amazing with coffee.

4 ounces milk chocolate

¼ cup heavy cream

1½ cups fresh lychees, peeled and seeded

Melt the chocolate. Add the cream and mix well. Dip the lychees in the chocolate. Place gently onto a paper-lined plate and let set in the fridge.

NOTE: You can use canned lychees—just drain and pat dry before dipping.

Chocolate Mousse Patty Cakes

MAKES 6

Recipe from Wendy King.

8 ounces milk chocolate

3 eggs

¼ cup GF self-rising flour

1¼ cups heavy cream, whipped, for serving

Preheat the oven to 350°F. Line 6 muffin cups with paper liners. In a saucepan, melt the chocolate over very low heat, stirring often until smooth. In a bowl, whisk together the eggs and flour. Stir into the chocolate. Spoon the batter into the muffin cups and bake for 20 minutes, or until the sides are set but the center is still liquid. Cool for 10 minutes. Carefully remove the paper. The centers will have a warm mousse consistency. Serve with whipped cream.

OPTIONAL: Sprinkle shaved chocolate on the whipped cream to make them look even more dazzling!

Chocolate Panna Cotta

MAKES 4

So smooooooooooooooooooooth!

1¼ cups heavy cream

7 ounces good-quality dark chocolate, chopped

½ envelope (0.25 ounce) unflavored gelatin

1 teaspoon vanilla extract

Grease four ½-cup ramekins and place on a baking sheet. In a small saucepan, heat the cream over medium heat for 1 to 2 minutes, or until just boiling. Remove from the heat and stir in the chocolate until nice and smooth. Mix the gelatin into 2 tablespoons boiling water and stir until dissolved. Stir the gelatin and vanilla into the cream mixture. Pour into the ramekins. Cover with plastic wrap and chill for at least 4 hours. To serve, briefly dip the base of the mold in warm water and turn out onto dessert plates.

Chocolate-Rum Cherries

MAKES 30

30 glacé cherries

¼ cup dark rum

4 ounces dark chocolate, chopped

½ cup pecans or walnuts, finely chopped

Combine the cherries and rum in a bowl and let stand overnight. In a microwaveable bowl, melt the chocolate in 15-second increments, stirring well after each. Drain the cherries and pat dry. Coat each cherry in the chocolate. Let sit for 1 minute, then sprinkle with the nuts. Refrigerate until set.

Citrus Frosting

MAKES 1 CUP

3 tablespoons cream cheese, at room temperature

1 tablespoon butter, at room temperature

1 teaspoon grated lemon zest

1 to 1½ cups GF confectioners' sugar

In a small bowl, beat together the cream cheese and butter. Add the lemon zest and 1 cup confectioners' sugar. Add more confectioners' sugar a little at a time to achieve spreading consistency. Beat until the icing is nice and smooth.

OPTIONAL: Substitute orange zest for lemon.

Cookies & Cream Truffles

MAKES 24

Watch these fly!

6 ounces GF chocolate cream cookies (Oreo imitation)

4 ounces cream cheese

8 ounces dark chocolate

4 ounces white chocolate

In a food processor, crush the cookies. Add the cream cheese, processing until there are no traces of cream cheese. Roll the mixture into small balls, place on a plate, and refrigerate for 45 minutes. Melt the dark chocolate in a bowl set over a pan of simmering water. When melted, roll the balls in the chocolate mixture to coat. Refrigerate until set. Melt the white chocolate the same way as the dark, and when nice and smooth, use a fork to dip and drizzle the white chocolate over the dark for an impressive finish.

OPTIONAL: You can use GF chocolate chip or plain chocolate cookies.

Cranberry Cookies

MAKES 12

2 cups GF pancake mix

½ cup whole milk

1 cup sugar

1 cup dried cranberries

Preheat the oven to 400°F. Line a baking sheet with parchment paper. Mix all the ingredients, then drop by spoonfuls onto the baking sheet. Bake for 10 to 12 minutes, or until just turning brown.

NOTE: These tend to cook faster than normal flour cookies.

OPTIONAL: Substitute chocolate chips for the cranberries.

Dark Chocolate Raspberry Fondue

SERVES 6 TO 8

15 ounces dark chocolate, coarsely chopped

About ⅔ cup heavy cream

2 ounces raspberries, pureed

¼ cup raspberry jam

In a medium microwaveable bowl, combine the chocolate, ⅔ cup cream, and the pureed raspberries. Microwave on medium-high in 30-second increments, stirring well after each, until the mixture is nice and smooth. Stir in the jam. Add more cream if the mixture seems too thick for dipping. Pour into a serving bowl or fondue pot to serve.

OPTIONAL: Serve with chopped croissants or ciabatta or fresh fruit to dip.

Energy Bars

MAKES 8

1 cup dates, chopped

¾ cup crunchy peanut butter

⅔ cup shredded coconut

2 tablespoons cocoa powder

In a blender, whiz all the ingredients until combined. Spoon into an 11 by 7-inch baking pan and gently press to smooth the surface. Refrigerate for at least 1 hour. Cut into 8 slices and wrap individually in plastic wrap or foil until ready to eat.

Espresso Amaretti

MAKES 24

1 tablespoon instant coffee

3 egg whites

1 cup superfine sugar

3 cups almond meal

Preheat the oven to 325°F. Line a baking sheet with parchment paper. Dissolve the coffee in 2 tablespoons boiling water. Let the mixture cool. With an electric mixer, beat the egg whites until stiff peaks form. Add the egg whites, sugar, and almond meal to the coffee mix and stir until combined. Using a tablespoon, dollop the mixture into mounds on the baking sheet. Bake for 20 minutes, or until just beginning to turn brown.

Flourless Chocolate Cake

SERVES 8

This cake collapses (as it has no flour to sustain the rise), but is dense and rich.

4 eggs, separated

1 cup superfine sugar

1¾ sticks (7 ounces) butter

8 ounces dark chocolate

Put a rack in the lowest position and preheat the oven to 350°F. Line a 9-inch round cake pan with parchment paper. With an electric mixer, beat the egg yolks with ½ cup of the sugar. In a separate bowl, beat the egg whites until fluffy, then add the remaining ½ cup sugar, gradually beating until stiff peaks form. In a bowl set over a pan of hot water, melt the butter and chocolate, stirring regularly. Fold the chocolate mixture into the egg yolks. Fold in the egg whites. Scrape the batter into the cake pan and bake for 40 minutes. Serve warm or chilled.

OPTIONAL: This is delicious with freshly whipped cream and a few fresh raspberries.

Frozen Fruit Yogurt Soft Serve

SERVES 4 TO 6

A recipe from Cyndi O'Meara.

2 cups coarsely chopped fresh fruit (bananas, strawberries, mango, blueberries, etc.)

½ cup honey

16 ounces plain yogurt

In a blender, process the fruit until smooth. Add the honey and yogurt and mix thoroughly. Pour into a covered container and freeze. Remove from the freezer 20 to 30 minutes before serving.

Fruit Bars

MAKES 12

13 ounces mixed dried fruit

1 can (14 ounces) condensed milk

1¼ cups GF self-rising flour

Preheat the oven to 325°F. Line a 12 by 8-inch baking pan with parchment paper. Mix all the ingredients together and spoon into the baking pan. Bake for 40 to 45 minutes, or until nice and golden on top. Let cool before cutting. Can be kept in the freezer for up to 1 month.

OPTIONAL: For a flavor variation, add 1 cup shredded coconut to the mixture before baking. This is lovely frosted with your favorite icing.

Fruitcake

SERVES 8

Recipe from Jen Whittington. S.e.n.s.a.t.i.o.n.a.l!

2¼ pounds mixed dried fruit

2 cups fruit juice or cold organic tea of choice

2 cups GF self-rising flour

Soak the fruit in the juice or tea overnight. Put a rack in the lowest position and preheat the oven to 250°F. Line a 9-inch round cake pan with parchment paper. Stir the flour into the soaked fruit (do not drain) and mix well. Spoon the mixture into the cake pan. Bake for 2 to 2½ hours, or until a toothpick inserted into the center of the cake comes out clean or with only a few crumbs clinging to it. Remove from the oven and let cool. Store in an airtight container; this cake will last in a cool place for up to 1 month. It's also suitable for freezing.

OPTIONAL: Add a shot of your favorite tipple—sherry, brandy, rum, or Grand Marnier.

Hazelnut Torte

SERVES 8

12 ounces skinned hazelnuts

2 teaspoons GF baking powder

6 eggs, separated

½ cup superfine sugar

Preheat the oven to 325°F. Line a 9-inch springform pan with parchment paper. Set aside about 10 hazelnuts if you wish to decorate (see box below) and put the rest in a blender and process until very fine. Add the baking powder and set aside. In a large bowl, beat the egg yolks with the sugar until pale yellow. Beat the ground hazelnut mixture into the egg yolk and sugar mixture. In another bowl, whisk the egg whites until stiff peaks form. Quickly fold one-third of the egg whites into the yolk mixture, then add the remaining whites and fold in until no streaks remain. Pour into the pan and bake for 1 hour to 1¼ hours, or until the top of the cake springs back when lightly touched.

OPTIONAL: When cool, split horizontally and spread generously with whipped cream. Decorate with strawberries or coffee cream (see the optional variation on Mascarpone Icing, page 185). Sprinkle with the reserved nuts.

Macarons

MAKES 16

Delicious individually or joined together with your favorite frosting.

2¼ cups confectioners' sugar

2 cups almond flour

5 egg whites

2 tablespoons granulated sugar

Preheat the oven to 200°F. Line a baking sheet with parchment paper. In a medium bowl, combine the confectioners' sugar and almond flour. In a separate clean, dry bowl, beat the egg whites until soft peaks form. Slowly add the granulated sugar and continue to beat until stiff peaks form. Sift one-third of the almond flour mixture into the egg whites and fold gently to combine. Sift in the remaining almond flour in two batches. Fully incorporate the ingredients, but be careful not to overfold. Spoon the mixture into a pastry bag fitted with a plain ½-inch tip. (You can also use a ziplock bag with a corner cut off.) Pipe 1-inch mounds onto the baking sheet. Bake for 5 minutes, remove the sheet from the oven, and raise the temperature to 375°F. Return the sheet to the oven and bake for an additional 7 to 8 minutes, or until the macarons are lightly colored. Cool on a rack.

Mascarpone Icing

MAKES 1 CUP

This is sensational on Walnut Cake (page 197). Yummy!!

½ cup heavy cream

4 ounces mascarpone

2 tablespoons GF confectioners' sugar

1 teaspoon honey

With a handheld mixer, mix all the ingredients until thick and creamy.

OPTIONAL: Replace the honey with fresh raspberries or blueberries, or with 1 tablespoon instant coffee for coffee cream.

Orange Coconut Clusters

MAKES 12

7 ounces dark chocolate

1 teaspoon orange extract

1 cup almonds, toasted and coarsely chopped

1 cup shredded coconut, toasted

Line a baking sheet with parchment paper. In a medium saucepan, melt the chocolate over very low heat. Stir in the orange extract. Cool slightly, then add the almonds and coconut. Stir to coat. Drop by heaping tablespoons onto the baking sheet. Refrigerate to set.

Orange Ricotta Puddings

MAKES 4

These are fabulous!

1¼ cups ricotta cheese

1 cup superfine sugar

½ cup heavy cream

2 oranges

In a bowl, beat the ricotta and sugar until smooth. Add the cream, the juice of 1 orange, and 2 tablespoons orange zest, beating until well combined. Spoon into serving bowls or glasses. Peel the remaining orange and separate into segments. Top each serving with orange segments. Refrigerate for at least 30 minutes before serving.

Pavlova

SERVES 6 TO 8

4 egg whites

1 cup superfine sugar

2 tablespoons cornstarch

1 teaspoon vanilla extract

Preheat the oven to 300°F. Line a baking sheet with parchment paper. Draw a 9-inch circle on the paper. In a large bowl, beat the egg whites until stiff. Gradually add the sugar, 1 tablespoon at a time, beating well after each addition. Beat until thick and glossy. Gently fold in the cornstarch and vanilla. Spoon the mixture within the circle, shaping it into a high mound. Bake for 1 hour, turn off the heat, open the oven door, and let the Pavlova cool in the oven.

OPTIONAL: Serve topped with freshly whipped cream and seasonal fruits or berries.

Peanut Butter Cookies

MAKES 24

1 cup crunchy peanut butter

1 cup packed brown sugar

1 teaspoon ground cinnamon

1 egg

Preheat the oven to 350°F. Line 2 baking sheets with parchment paper. In a bowl, mix all the ingredients. Using tablespoon amounts, roll into small balls and place on the baking sheets. Flatten slightly with a fork, crisscross style. Bake for 10 minutes, or until a thin crust forms on the cookie.

NOTE: These will harden as they cool.

Peanut Butter Ice Cream Pie

SERVES 6 TO 8

7 ounces GF chocolate chip cookies, finely crumbled

6 tablespoons butter, melted

1 quart creamy vanilla ice cream, softened

1¼ cups crunchy peanut butter

In a bowl, mix the cookie crumbs and butter. Press into a parchment paper–lined pie dish and chill. With an electric mixer, beat the ice cream and peanut butter until nice and smooth. Pour into the chilled pie shell and freeze for at least 3 hours before serving.

OPTIONAL: Serve drizzled with Hot Fudge Sauce (page 15).

Pears in Coffee Syrup

SERVES 4

These are easy and economical, especially when in season.

½ cup sugar

2 teaspoons instant coffee

4 pears, peeled

In a saucepan, combine the sugar and coffee with 2 cups water and stir over low heat until the sugar is dissolved. Add the pears and simmer until they are soft. To serve, place the pears in individual bowls and pour the syrup around them.

Quart Cake

SERVES 8

Recipe from Peter in the BBC studios in London.

3 eggs

2 sticks (8 ounces) butter, softened

1 cup muscovado sugar

1 cup GF self-rising flour

Preheat the oven to 350°F. Line a 9 by 5 by 3-inch loaf pan with parchment paper. Mix all the ingredients together and scrape the batter into the loaf pan. Bake for 45 minutes.

Raisin Loaf

SERVES 8

A fantastic recipe from the quirky Kt Anbeck.
Cut into thick slices and serve with butter.

1 tablespoon butter, plus extra for greasing the pan

1 cup sugar

1 cup raisins

2 cups GF self-rising flour

Preheat the oven to 350°F. Butter a 9 by 5 by 3-inch loaf pan. In a saucepan, combine the 1 tablespoon butter, the sugar, raisins, and 1 cup water. Bring to a boil, reduce to a simmer, and cook for 5 minutes. Set aside and let cool. Stir in the flour until well blended. Scrape the batter into the loaf pan and bake for 45 minutes.

Raspberry & Almond Cake

SERVES 12

Topped with cream cheese icing and sprinkled with poppy seeds,
this cake is BEEEEUUUUUUUTIFUL!!

2 cups frozen raspberries, thawed (juice reserved)

6 eggs

1 cup superfine sugar

2¼ cups almond meal

Preheat the oven to 325°F. Grease a 9-inch round cake pan. In a blender, puree the raspberries with their juice; don't strain out the seeds. In a bowl, beat the eggs and sugar with an electric mixer until light and fluffy. Add the raspberry puree and almond meal and stir well. Pour the batter into the cake pan and bake for 1 hour to 1 hour and 10 minutes.

OPTIONAL: You can substitute apples, bananas, oranges, or mandarin oranges for the raspberries.

Raspberry Tofu Mousse

SERVES 4

1 pint fresh raspberries
(reserve some for garnish)

12 ounces silken tofu

½ teaspoon vanilla extract

3 tablespoons honey

Combine all the ingredients and blend well. Divide the mixture among 4 shallow dessert dishes and chill for 2 hours. Garnish with the reserved raspberries and serve.

Roasted Honey Pears with Honey Cream

SERVES 4

3 firm-ripe pears, quartered and cored

½ cup honey

2 tablespoons light brown sugar

1¼ cups heavy cream, whipped

Preheat the oven to 350°F. Place the pears in a baking dish. Drizzle with ¼ cup of the honey and sprinkle with the brown sugar. Pour ½ cup water around the pears. Bake, uncovered, for 30 minutes, or until just soft. Place 3 pear quarters on each of 4 dessert plates. Drizzle the pan juices over the pears. Mix the whipped cream and the remaining ¼ cup honey together until combined. Serve over the pears.

OPTIONAL: Add ¼ teaspoon cinnamon to the whipped cream for a lovely flavor.

Rocky Road

MAKES 12

A recipe by Jennette McCosker. Kim's favorite!!

8 ounces GF milk chocolate, broken into pieces

4 ounces macadamia nuts, coarsely chopped

1 cup GF marshmallows

1 cup GF Turkish delight, coarsely chopped

In a microwaveable bowl, melt the chocolate in 20-second increments, stirring well after each. Let cool slightly, then stir in the remaining ingredients, mixing until well combined. Line a 13 by 9-inch rectangular dish with parchment paper, pour the mixture into it, neaten the edges, and refrigerate until set. Cut into desired serving pieces.

OPTIONAL: Use any nut of choice—almonds, hazelnuts, Brazil nuts, etc.

Rum Raisin Ice Cream

SERVES 8

1 cup raisins

½ cup dark rum

½ gallon GF creamy vanilla ice cream, softened

In a saucepan, combine the raisins and rum and bring to a simmer over medium heat. Remove from the heat and let cool completely. In a food processor, process the raisin mixture until roughly chopped. Fold into the container of ice cream. Cover with plastic wrap, seal with the lid of the container, and freeze overnight before serving.

Shortbread

MAKES 16

1 cup rice flour

½ cup cornstarch

½ cup GF confectioners' sugar

1½ sticks (6 ounces) butter, at room temperature

Sift the rice flour and cornstarch into a bowl. Add the sugar and butter and mix with your hands until a soft dough forms. Roll into a 2-inch-thick log and refrigerate for 1 hour. Preheat the oven to 350°F. Line a baking sheet with parchment paper. Remove the dough from the fridge and cut into ¼-inch-thick slices. Arrange on the baking sheet, allowing room for spreading. Bake for 20 to 25 minutes, or until golden.

OPTIONAL: Sprinkle with superfine sugar before baking. Or roll into ¾-inch balls, and at Christmastime press half a glazed cherry onto each ball before baking.

Soy Custard

SERVES 4

5 egg yolks

1 cup pure maple syrup

2 cups GF soy milk

In a bowl, whisk together the egg yolks and maple syrup. In a saucepan, warm the soy milk. Add the egg and maple mixture to the milk. Return the saucepan to medium heat and stir constantly until the mixture thickens.

Sponge Cake

SERVES 8

¾ cup cornstarch

1 teaspoon GF baking powder

3 eggs, separated

½ cup superfine sugar

Preheat the oven to 350°F. Line an 8-inch square cake pan with parchment paper. Sift the cornstarch and baking powder with a pinch of salt. With an electric mixer, beat the egg whites until stiff peaks start to form. Beat in the egg yolks. Gradually beat in the sugar until the mixture is light, beating for about 10 minutes. Fold in the dry ingredients with a whisk (helps to keep the mixture aerated). Pour the batter into the pan and bake for 20 to 25 minutes. Remove from the pan and cool on a rack.

OPTIONAL: Serve topped with whipped cream and chopped strawberries.

Sticky Mango Rice

SERVES 6

This is delectable!

1 cup short-grain rice

½ cup sugar

1 can (12 ounces) coconut cream

3 mangoes, sliced

In a saucepan, combine the rice and 1¾ cups water and bring to a boil. Reduce the heat, cover, and cook about 10 minutes. Stir in the sugar and 1 cup of the coconut cream and cook, stirring, until the rice is nice and soft. Dollop the mixture into serving bowls and top with mango slices drizzled with the remaining coconut cream.

OPTIONAL: Substitute lychees for mangoes.

Strawberry & Banana Skewers with Caramel Sauce

MAKES 12

Loved by all!

1 can (13 to 14 ounces) dulce de leche

⅓ cup heavy cream

1 quart strawberries

2 bananas, sliced

In a saucepan, combine the dulce de leche and cream and bring to a boil. Reduce to a simmer and cook for 2 to 3 minutes. Pour the mixture into a pitcher and let cool. Thread the strawberries and bananas alternately onto 12 skewers. Drizzle with the sauce when ready to serve.

Stuffed Apples

MAKES 4

YUMMMMMMY!!! Great served with GF custard or heavy cream.

4 large Granny Smith apples

4 ounces leftover GF fruitcake

Preheat the oven to 350°F. Core the apples, wrap in foil, and bake for 20 minutes. Remove the foil and stuff the apples with the fruitcake. Bake for 10 minutes longer. Serve warm.

OPTIONAL: Sprinkle with cinnamon or substitute raisins for fruitcake, as Kim's nana, Mary Moore, has been doing for decades!

Sweet Pastry

SERVES 6

This is good for sweet pies, tarts, and cheesecakes.

½ cup cornstarch

¾ cup whole milk

1½ cups shredded coconut

8 tablespoons (1 stick) butter, melted

Mix everything together and press into a pie plate.

Tropical Fruit Salad

SERVES 4

Simply scrumptious! Delicious served with ice cream or as an accompaniment to a sweet.

1 mango, diced

8 lychees, peeled and quartered

1 banana, sliced

3 passion fruits

Combine all and mix.

Walnut Cake

SERVES 8

This is brilliant!

4 eggs, separated

1 cup superfine sugar

Grated zest of 1 lemon

12 ounces walnuts, finely ground

Preheat the oven to 325°F. Line a 9-inch springform pan with parchment paper. With an electric mixer, beat the egg yolks and sugar together until light and fluffy, about 5 minutes. Beat in the lemon zest. In a separate bowl, beat the egg whites until stiff peaks form. Fold one-third of the whites into the yolk mixture. Add the ground walnuts, stirring until thoroughly blended. Carefully fold in the remaining egg whites to maintain a light texture. Pour the mixture into the pan and bake for 50 to 60 minutes, or until firm and golden brown. Let cool in the pan.

OPTIONAL: Serve with freshly made Mascarpone Icing (page 185).

White Choc Macaroons

MAKES 16

2 eggs, separated

¾ cup superfine sugar

2 cups shredded coconut

1 cup coarsely grated white chocolate

Preheat the oven to 325°F. With an electric mixer, beat the egg whites until soft peaks form. Gradually beat in the egg yolks and then the sugar, beating until the sugar has dissolved. Stir in the coconut and chocolate. Roll into balls using 2 teaspoons per ball and place 1 inch apart on a nonstick baking sheet. Bake for 20 minutes, or until golden brown. Let cool on the pan for 5 minutes before transferring to a rack to cool completely.

OPTIONAL: Rachel Kelly suggested substituting the zest of a lime for the white chocolate, making Coconut & Lime Macaroons!

DRINKS

It usually takes a long time to find a shorter way.

—Anonymous

Apple Citrus Refresher

SERVES 4

2 Granny Smith apples, chopped

2 oranges, peeled and sectioned

Juice of 1 small lime

2 cups ginger ale

In an electric juicer, juice the apples and oranges. Pour the juice into a pitcher. Stir in the lime juice and refrigerate. Just before serving, stir in the ginger ale. Serve in tall glasses over stacks of crushed ice.

Banana Fruit Frappé

SERVES 3

1 cup pineapple juice

3 bananas, sliced

1 tablespoon honey

2 cups ice

Combine all the ingredients in a blender and puree until smooth.

Berry Blast

SERVES 2

Serve this in glasses or pour it over pancakes, crepes, or ice cream. Recipe by Sue Edmondstone.

4 ounces frozen strawberries (or chilled fresh strawberries)

2 ounces blueberries

2 guavas, peeled

Juice of 2 oranges

Combine all the ingredients in a blender and puree until smooth. Serve immediately.

Energizer Drink

SERVES 2

2 carrots

½-inch piece fresh ginger

2 celery stalks

2 oranges, peeled and
sectioned

In an electric juicer, juice all the
ingredients. Serve over crushed ice.

Jumpin' Ginger Juice

SERVES 4

A recipe by Marie McColl.

2 oranges

3 tablespoons black currant
syrup

5 cups ginger ale

Juice 1½ oranges and cut the other
½ orange into thin wedges. Blend
together the orange juice, syrup, ginger
ale, and several ice cubes. Garnish with
the orange wedges.

Muesli Smoothie

SERVES 1 OR 2

A recipe from the lovely Kim Morrison.

1 cup milk or GF soy milk

1 frozen banana

½ cup GF toasted muesli

3 tablespoons fruit yogurt

Put all the ingredients into a blender and
whiz until smooth.

OPTIONAL: Add ice if you would like it colder.

Pink Slushies

SERVES 2

A recipe from Georgia Darr and Maddie Willson.

4 cups cubed watermelon

3 tablespoons fresh lime juice

⅔ cup orange juice

¼ cup sugar

In a blender, combine all the ingredients. Fill with ice and blend until smooth. Pour into 4 tall glasses and serve.

Strawberry Lemonade

SERVES 4

1 cup sugar

4 lemons

8 ounces strawberries, quartered

In a saucepan, stir the sugar and 2 cups water over low heat until the sugar dissolves. Simmer for 5 minutes. Grate the zest of 2 lemons, then juice them all. Add 3 cups water, the lemon juice, and the zest to the saucepan. Pour into a large pitcher. Add the strawberries and chill. Serve over lots of crushed ice.

Tor's Piña Colada

SERVES 4

A Samoan staple!

1 cup crushed pineapple

1 can (14 ounces) coconut cream

1 cup whole milk

Combine all the ingredients in a blender and puree until smooth. Serve over crushed ice.

Tropical Delight

SERVES 2

Recipe by Majella Coleman.

1 cup cubed fresh pineapple

1 banana

8 ounces passion fruit yogurt

2 tablespoons honey

Combine all the ingredients in a blender and puree until smooth. Serve with a few ice cubes.

Virgin Mary

MAKES 1

1 cup tomato juice

1 tablespoon fresh lemon juice

1 teaspoon GF Worcestershire sauce

4 drops Tabasco sauce

Mix all the ingredients in a pitcher. Pour into a tall glass with crushed ice.

OPTIONAL: Serve garnished with a trimmed celery stalk.

FOR THE CHILDREN

*The best thing a father can do for his children
is to love their mother!*

—Unknown

ALL I REALLY NEED TO KNOW I LEARNED IN KINDERGARTEN

(A Guide for Global Leadership)
An excerpt from the book
All I Really Need to Know I Learned in Kindergarten,
by Robert Fulghum
www.robertfulghum.com

All I really need to know about how to live, and what to do, and how to be, I learned in kindergarten. Wisdom was not at the top of the graduate school mountain, but there in the sand pile at Sunday school. These are the things I learned:

- Share everything.
- Play fair.
- Don't hit people.
- Put things back where you found them.
- Clean up your own mess.
- Don't take things that are not yours.
- Say you're sorry when you hurt somebody.
- Wash your hands before you eat.
- Flush.
- Warm cookies and cold milk are good for you.
- Live a balanced life—learn some and think some and draw and paint and sing and dance and play and work every day some.
- Take a nap every afternoon.
- When you go out in the world, watch out for traffic, hold hands, and stick together.
- Be aware of wonder. Remember the little seed in the Styrofoam cup: the roots go down and the plant goes up and nobody really knows how or why, but we are all like that.

- Goldfish and hamsters and white mice and even the little seed in the Styrofoam cup—they all die. So do we.
- And then remember the Dick-and-Jane books and the first word you learned—the biggest word of all—*LOOK!*

Take any one of those items and extrapolate it into sophisticated adult terms and apply it to your family life or your work or government or your world and it holds true and clear and firm.

Think what a better world it would be if we all—*the whole world*—had cookies and milk at about 3 o'clock in the afternoon and then lay down with our blankies for a nap. Or if all governments had as a basic policy to always put things back where they found them and to clean up their own mess.

And it is still true, no matter how old you are, when you go out in the world, it is best to hold hands and stick together!

BBQ Chicken Pizza

MAKES 2

2 GF wraps (8-inch)

4 tablespoons GF barbecue sauce

8 ounces roasted chicken, shredded

½ cup shredded mozzarella cheese

Preheat the oven to 350°F. Spread the wraps with the sauce. Top with the chicken and sprinkle with the mozzarella. Bake for 10 minutes, or until the cheese is melted and lightly browned.

OPTIONAL FILLINGS: For "Meat Lover's Pizza," add ham and finely chopped bacon. For "Funghi Pizza," add thinly sliced mushrooms and substitute pizza sauce for the barbecue sauce. For "Vegetarian Pizza," omit the chicken and add a selection of antipasti. Put it on a pizza and they will eat it!

Chicken Carnival Cones

MAKES 8

A recipe by Isobele "Pruuuu" Whiting that is enjoyed by everyone!

8 GF tortillas (8-inch)

2 cups shredded leftover chicken

1 cup salsa

4 ounces Cheddar cheese, grated

Preheat the oven to 350°F. Line a baking sheet with parchment paper. Fold the bottom third of each tortilla up, pinch it in the middle of the base, and fold it around itself, forming a cone. Fill the bottom of the cone with chicken, dollop 2 tablespoons of salsa over it, then cover with a layer of Cheddar. Place on the baking sheet. Repeat the process until all the ingredients are used. Bake for 15 minutes.

Chicken, Mango & Chickpea Burgers

MAKES 12

1 can (15 ounces) chickpeas, rinsed and drained

1 pound ground chicken breast

4 or 5 tablespoons GF mango chutney

2 scallions, finely chopped

In a food processor or blender, chop the chickpeas coarsely. In a bowl, combine the chickpeas with the chicken, chutney, scallions, and salt and pepper to taste. Shape into patties. In a nonstick skillet, cook the patties over medium heat for 3 minutes on one side. Flip and cook for 3 minutes, or until cooked through.

OPTIONAL: Serve on a roll with lettuce and a slice of tomato.

Chicken Nuggets # 1

SERVES 4

¾ cup yellow cornmeal

1 teaspoon dried sage

1 pound skinless, boneless chicken breasts, cut into bite-size pieces

½ cup peanut oil

In a plastic bag, combine the cornmeal and sage. Add the chicken and toss to coat evenly. In a nonstick skillet, heat the oil until really hot. Add the coated chicken and cook for about 1 minute per side. Use extra oil if needed.

Chicken Nuggets # 2

SERVES 4

½ cup GF mayonnaise

1 cup instant GF potato flakes

1 pound skinless, boneless chicken breasts, cut into bite-size pieces

Preheat the oven to 400°F. Line a baking sheet with parchment paper. Place the mayonnaise and potato flakes on 2 separate plates. Roll the chicken first in the mayonnaise and then in the potato flakes. Place the coated pieces on the baking sheet and bake for 20 minutes, flipping once, until browned on both sides and cooked through.

Chicken Patties

MAKES 10

3 slices GF white bread, grated

1 pound ground chicken

1¼ cups shredded mozzarella cheese

1 egg yolk

In a large bowl, combine all the ingredients. Form into patties. In a nonstick skillet, cook the patties until golden on both sides.

Creamy Meatballs

SERVES 4 TO 6

1¾ pounds extra-lean ground beef

1 cup sour cream

1 teaspoon garlic salt

2 tablespoons olive oil

In a bowl, combine the beef, sour cream, and garlic salt. Roll into meatballs. In a nonstick skillet, heat the oil over medium heat. Add the meatballs and cook until browned all over.

OPTIONAL: Roll in GF bread crumbs before frying.

Easy Pork Bites

MAKES 36

A recipe from the brilliant Michelle Dodd.

6 GF flavored sausages (see Note), casings removed

Preheat the oven to 350°F. Roll the sausage meat into bite-size balls and bake for 15 minutes. Serve warm with your favorite sauce.

NOTE: For the sausages, use Italian, herb and garlic, honey and rosemary, rosemary and lamb . . . whatever strikes your fancy!

Fish Pie

SERVES 4

A Turnbull household staple. Yummy! This is delicious served with a variety of fresh steamed veggies.

4 potatoes, peeled and cut into chunks

1¼ cups GF tomato and basil pasta sauce

4 white fish fillets, cut into chunks

4 ounces Cheddar cheese, grated

In a large saucepan of boiling water, cook the potatoes until tender. Drain and mash. Preheat the broiler. In a nonstick skillet, heat the sauce over medium heat. Add the fish and cook for 8 minutes, or until the fish is done. Remove from the heat. Transfer to a 13 by 9-inch baking dish and spread with the mashed potatoes. Sprinkle with the Cheddar. Broil until the cheese has melted and turned a lovely golden color.

Healthy Hot Dogs

SERVES 4

4 GF hot dogs

4 GF wraps (8-inch)

4 ounces Cheddar cheese, grated

1 carrot, grated

Broil or grill the hot dogs. Sprinkle the wraps with the Cheddar and carrot. Top each wrap with a hot dog and roll up.

OPTIONAL: Serve with GF ketchup or GF barbecue sauce.

Honey Drummies

SERVES 2

Recipe from mighty mummy Michelle Ashdown.
Serve with veggies or rice.

4 chicken drumsticks

2 tablespoons honey

2 tablespoons pear juice

1 teaspoon olive oil

Place the chicken drumsticks in an airtight container. Combine the honey, pear juice, oil, and ½ teaspoon sea salt. Pour over the chicken and marinate for 4 hours. Preheat the oven to 350°F. Line a baking sheet with parchment paper. Arrange the chicken on the baking sheet and bake for 40 minutes. Spoon the juices over the chicken twice during the baking.

Hot Dog Pasta Bake

SERVES 4 TO 6

6 GF hot dogs, quartered

2 cups cooked GF pasta spirals

1½ cups GF pasta sauce

1 cup grated Parmesan cheese

Preheat the oven to 350°F. Mix the hot dogs, pasta, and sauce together and spoon into a baking dish. Sprinkle with the Parmesan. Bake for 20 minutes.

Hummus Sausages

SERVES 2

Soooooo quick and easy—recipe by the very suave Tony Van Dijk.

4 GF herbed or Italian
sausages

4 teaspoons hummus

1 lemon, quartered

Broil or panfry the sausages and serve with a dollop of hummus and a lemon wedge.

Lasagna

SERVES 4 TO 6

Recipe by Dan Primmer.

1 pound ground beef

2 cups GF pasta sauce

6 GF lasagna sheets

4 ounces mozzarella cheese, grated

Preheat the oven to 350°F. In a nonstick skillet, cook the beef over low heat. When browned, add the pasta sauce and simmer; season with salt and pepper to taste. Spoon half the beef sauce into a 13 by 9-inch baking dish. Top with 3 *dampened* lasagna sheets. Sprinkle with the mozzarella. Repeat the layering. Press gently to be sure the pasta sheets are in contact with the liquid. Cover with foil and bake for 45 to 50 minutes, or until the pasta has softened.

NOTE: We often buy ground beef in 4-pound quantities to get the "buy in bulk" discount. We ask our butchers to pack it in 1-pound lots, as that is what suits our families' needs.

Mini Cheese Quiches

SERVES 4

4 GF tortillas (10-inch)

½ cup grated Cheddar cheese

1 tablespoon mixed herbs

2 eggs, lightly beaten

Preheat the oven to 400°F. Using a large biscuit cutter, cut out 3 rounds from each tortilla. Line 12 cups of a nonstick muffin tin with the tortilla rounds (dampen slightly to help mold if necessary). Fill each cup with Cheddar and herbs and add a sprinkle of pepper. Top each with some egg and bake for 15 minutes, or until set.

Mousetraps

SERVES 1

Recipe by Wendy King.

2 slices day-old GF bread

2 slices Cheddar cheese

1 slice GF bacon, cut in half

Preheat the broiler. Cut the crusts off the bread and place the bread on a broiler pan. Lay a slice of cheese on each piece of bread and top with a piece of bacon. Broil until the bacon is crispy. Cut each slice into 3 fingers.

Peanut Butter Toasties

SERVES 2

2 slices GF bread

2 tablespoons peanut butter

2 tablespoons raisins

2 tablespoons shredded Cheddar cheese

Broil one side of the bread until golden. Flip and spread with the peanut butter. Sprinkle with the raisins and top with the Cheddar. Broil until the cheese is melted. Cut in half to serve.

Potato Bake

SERVES 2 TO 4

2 large potatoes, thinly sliced

½ cup heavy cream

½ cup whole milk

1 teaspoon grated nutmeg

Preheat the oven to 350°F. Grease a pie plate and layer with the potatoes. Mix the cream and milk and pour over the potatoes. Sprinkle with the nutmeg and bake for 30 to 40 minutes, or until golden brown.

Roma Chicken

SERVES 4

A recipe from Katrina Price. Your children will loooooove this! Serve over rice.

½ rotisserie chicken, skin removed

2 cups GF tomato-based pasta sauce

1 red bell pepper, sliced

2 tablespoons sour cream

Pull the chicken meat off the bone and shred. In a nonstick skillet, combine the chicken, sauce, bell pepper, and sea salt and pepper to taste. Simmer until the bell pepper is tender. Stir in the sour cream at the end.

Savory Muffins

MAKES 24 MINI OR 12 LARGE MUFFINS

Recipe by Dymphna Boholt.

2 cups GF self-rising flour

2 eggs

1¼ cups shredded Cheddar cheese

1 cup whole milk

Preheat the oven to 400°F. Mix all the ingredients together and divide among the cups of a mini muffin tin or a regular muffin tin. Bake for 17 minutes for mini muffins or 26 minutes for regular muffins.

Shepherd's Pie with a Twist

SERVES 6

Hamilton, seven, often asks for "pie" (meaning this) for dinner!

1 pound ground beef

1 can (15 ounces) GF spaghetti in tomato sauce

3 large potatoes, peeled, boiled, and mashed

⅔ cup shredded Cheddar cheese

Preheat the oven to 350°F. In a nonstick skillet, cook the beef until browned (drain any excess liquid). Stir in the spaghetti and sea salt and pepper, and simmer for 10 minutes. Transfer to a 9-inch square baking dish and top with the mashed potatoes and Cheddar. Bake for 15 minutes, or until the cheese is golden brown.

Tacos

MAKES 2

½ pound lean ground beef

1 cup GF pasta sauce

2 GF taco shells

1 cup shredded lettuce

In a nonstick skillet, cook the beef until no longer pink. Add the pasta sauce and simmer over low heat for 5 minutes. Fill the taco shells with alternating layers of beef and lettuce.

OPTIONAL: You can also add sliced mushrooms, peas, and shredded carrot to the beef mixture.

Yummy Bean Grill

MAKES 2

1 can (8 ounces) GF baked beans

1 tablespoon finely chopped parsley

2 slices GF bread, lightly toasted

2 thin slices mozzarella cheese

Preheat the broiler. Combine the beans and parsley and spread over the toast. Top with the mozzarella and broil until the cheese melts.

Apricot Dream Balls

MAKES 24

Paul Bermingham's favorites!

4 ounces mixed dried fruit

10 plump dried apricots

1 tablespoon coconut milk

½ cup shredded coconut

In a food processor, combine the mixed fruit, apricots, and coconut milk and process until the mixture comes together. Shape into balls and roll in the coconut. Chill until firm.

Caramel Cookies

MAKES 24

1¾ stick (7 ounces) butter, at room temperature

½ cup packed light brown sugar

2 tablespoons golden syrup (such as Lyle's) or dark corn syrup

1 cup GF self-rising flour

Preheat the oven to 350°F. Line a baking sheet with parchment paper. Cream the butter and brown sugar. Add the syrup and beat until fluffy. Mix in the flour until the texture is such that you are able to roll the dough into 2-inch balls. Place the balls on the baking sheet, leaving room for them to spread. Press each gently with a fork and bake for 15 minutes.

Chocolate Balls

MAKES 32

A recipe by Grandma McCosker and loved by Matthew, Brady, and Harry!

7 ounces GF vanilla cookies

3 tablespoons unsweetened cocoa or GF hot chocolate mix

¾ cup condensed milk

½ cup shredded coconut

In a blender, process the cookies until finely crushed. Transfer to a bowl and mix in the cocoa and condensed milk to make a thick, sticky consistency. Using a generous teaspoon of the mixture, roll into balls and cover in coconut. Chill before serving. These can also be frozen.

NOTE: Wet hands make rolling these much easier. If the dough is too sticky, add more cookie crumbles.

Chocolate-Dipped Fruit

SERVES 4

7 ounces chocolate melts

2 bananas, thickly sliced

8 ounces strawberries

¾ cup dried apricots

Line a baking sheet with parchment paper. In a microwaveable bowl, microwave the chocolate melts in 15-second increments, stirring after each, until melted. Dip the fruit, one piece at a time, halfway into the chocolate to coat. Place on the baking sheet and refrigerate until set.

Chocolate Marshmallow Truffles

MAKES 24

14 ounces chocolate chips

8 ounces GF marshmallows

2 ounces sliced almonds, finely chopped

Line a baking sheet with parchment paper. In a microwaveable bowl, melt the chocolate in 15-second increments, stirring after each. Dip the marshmallows one at a time into the melted chocolate, turning to coat evenly. Gently shake off any excess chocolate and place the marshmallows on the baking sheet. Sprinkle with the almonds. Refrigerate to set.

Chocolate Toffee

MAKES 24

2½ cups sugar

8 tablespoons (1 stick) butter

¼ teaspoon cream of tartar

4 ounces dark chocolate, finely chopped

Line a 24-cup mini muffin tin with paper liners. In a saucepan, combine the sugar, butter, and cream of tartar. Add 1 cup water and cook over medium heat, stirring constantly, until the sugar dissolves. Bring to a boil and cook for 2 to 3 minutes, then remove from the heat immediately and quickly stir in the chocolate. Pour the mixture into the muffin cups. Refrigerate to set.

Cupcakes

MAKES 24

Your children will devour these.

1 stick plus 1 tablespoon (4½ ounces) butter, at room temperature

¾ cup superfine sugar

3 eggs

2 cups GF self-rising flour

Preheat the oven to 325°F. Line 24 mini muffin cups with paper liners. With an electric mixer on low speed, beat the butter, sugar, eggs, flour, and ¼ cup water until just combined. Then beat on medium until the mixture is nice and smooth. Spoon the batter evenly into the liners and bake for 20 minutes.

OPTIONAL: Serve topped with your favorite frosting.

Egg Custard

MAKES 2 CUPS

Grandma McCosker used to make this with Prune Snow (page 230). Delicious!

2 cups whole milk

5 tablespoons superfine sugar

2 egg yolks

2 tablespoons cornstarch

In a saucepan, bring the milk and 2 tablespoons of the sugar to a boil over medium heat. In a bowl, whisk together the yolks and remaining 3 tablespoons sugar. Gradually fold in the cornstarch to form a pale yellow paste. Carefully pour half of the boiled milk into the yolk mixture, whisking to incorporate. Return the remaining milk to the heat and bring to a boil, then quickly whisk in the yolk mixture. Continue whisking until it returns to a boil. Transfer to a clean, dry bowl and cover the surface with plastic wrap. Chill until ready to serve.

NOTE: To use the custard once it has been chilled, beat until smooth. An electric mixer gives a much smoother result than beating by hand.

Fruit Dip

MAKES 1 CUP

Serve with a platter of fresh fruit for dipping.

1 cup Greek yogurt

½ teaspoon ground cinnamon

3 tablespoons fruit jam

Combine all the ingredients in a bowl and mix well. Chill for at least 2 hours before serving to allow the flavors time to develop.

Fruit Kebabs

SERVES 4 TO 6

6 strawberries

3 kiwifruits

¼ cantaloupe

½ watermelon

Wash and hull the strawberries, and cut in half. Peel and quarter the kiwifruits. Cut the cantaloupe and watermelon into bite-size cubes. Trim the sharp ends from bamboo skewers and thread 6 pieces of fruit onto each, alternating the strawberries, kiwifruits, cantaloupe, and watermelon to create a colorful presentation.

OPTIONAL: Serve with a bowl of creamy Greek yogurt drizzled with honey.

Fruit Medley

SERVES 8

4 nectarines, chopped

2 bananas, sliced

4 ounces blueberries

1 tablespoon orange juice

Combine all the ingredients in a bowl and gently toss. Chill in the fridge before serving.

Honey & Cornflake Cookies

MAKES 24

This is Jaxson's #1 favorite cookie!

1¼ sticks (5 ounces) butter

½ cup honey

2 cups GF self-rising flour

2½ cups GF cornflakes

Preheat the oven to 350°F. Line 2 baking sheets with parchment paper. In a small saucepan, combine the butter and honey and stir over low heat. In a bowl, combine the flour and cornflakes. Pour in the butter mixture and stir to combine. Using a tablespoon, roll the mixture into balls and place on the baking sheets. With a fork, flatten slightly. Bake for 10 minutes, or until golden. Let cool on the baking sheets.

NOTE: For best storage, layer in an airtight container with parchment paper between the layers.

Jam Drops

MAKES 60

Recipe by Joy Duke.

2 sticks (8 ounces) butter, at room temperature

½ cup superfine sugar

2 cups GF all-purpose flour

½ cup strawberry jam

Preheat the oven to 375°F. Line a baking sheet with parchment paper. Cream the butter and sugar until light and fluffy. Fold in the flour and roll into 2-inch balls. Place on the baking sheet. Use the end of a wooden spoon to push a hole almost through to the base of each dough ball. Fill the holes with jam and bake for 15 minutes, or until slightly golden. Let cool before serving.

Kisses

MAKES 24

8 tablespoons (1 stick) butter, at room temperature

1 tablespoon GF confectioners' sugar

1 cup GF self-rising flour

1 tablespoon arrowroot

Preheat the oven to 300°F. Line a baking sheet with parchment paper. With an electric mixer, cream the butter and sugar. Beat in the flour and arrowroot. Roll by the teaspoon into balls and place on the baking sheet. Press with a fork. Bake for 10 minutes, or until golden brown.

OPTIONAL: Join 2 kisses together with some jam or icing when cold.

Mallow Pears

MAKES 4

A recipe by Justine Ormsby.

2 pears, halved and cored

8 GF marshmallows (or lots of GF mini marshmallows)

¼ teaspoon grated nutmeg

Preheat the broiler to medium. Place the pear halves on a microwaveable plate, cover, and microwave for 1 minute. Transfer to a broiler pan and top each pear with 2 marshmallows and a sprinkle of nutmeg. Broil until the marshmallows are golden brown. Serve warm.

Melon Ice Blocks

MAKES 8

4 cups chopped seedless watermelon

2 cups chopped fresh pineapple

In batches in a blender, puree the fruits until smooth. Pour into ice cube trays and freeze.

OPTIONAL: Substitute 2 cups honeydew melon for the watermelon.

Muesli Bars

MAKES 12

8 tablespoons (1 stick) butter

3 cups GF muesli

½ cup golden syrup (such as Lyle's) or dark corn syrup

Line a 13 by 9-inch rimmed baking sheet with parchment paper. In a medium saucepan, melt the butter. Add the muesli and syrup, stirring over medium heat for about 5 minutes, or until the mixture thickens and is dark golden brown. Spread in the pan. Cover and refrigerate to set. Slice into bars.

Orange Delight

MAKES 2

Ideal for an after-school snack.

2 oranges

Insert a Popsicle stick into a peeled orange, wrap with plastic wrap, and freeze for 1 to 2 hours.

Peppermint Chocolate Slice

MAKES ABOUT 20 PIECES

This is BRILLIANT, and so very easy, the kids can do it!

7 ounces dark chocolate melts

3 drops peppermint extract

4 ounces white chocolate melts

4 drops green food coloring

Line an 8-inch square cake pan with parchment paper or foil. In a saucepan, melt the dark chocolate over very low heat, stirring constantly. Stir in the peppermint extract. Spread half the mixture evenly over the bottom of the pan. Refrigerate for 5 minutes to set. Melt the white chocolate the same way and stir in the green food coloring. Spread all of this over the layer of dark chocolate and refrigerate to set. Spread the remaining dark chocolate over the white/green chocolate and refrigerate to set. Cut into pieces and store in the fridge.

Prune Snow

SERVES 4

This is delicious served with Egg Custard (page 224).

1 cup pitted prunes

2 egg whites

2 tablespoons superfine sugar

Place the prunes in a saucepan and cover with water. Cook for about 10 minutes, or until soft. Remove from the heat, drain, and let cool. Meanwhile, beat the egg whites until fluffy. Add the sugar gradually and continue to beat until stiff peaks form. Mash the prunes and fold into the egg whites.

Rice Pudding

SERVES 4

A recipe from the beautiful Mary Moore, great-grandmother to sixteen.

4 cups milk

½ cup medium-grain rice

2 tablespoons sugar

½ teaspoon vanilla extract

Preheat the oven to 300°F. Combine all the ingredients in a 9-inch square baking dish and bake in the middle of the oven for 1½ hours.

Rocky Road Ice Cream

SERVES 8

A fantastic version from the wonderful Wendy Beattie.

7 ounces GF chocolate cookies, chopped

7 ounces GF marshmallows, cut into small bits

1 cup GF red raspberry jelly candies

½ gallon GF chocolate ice cream, softened

In a large bowl, stir the first 3 ingredients into the ice cream. Pour the mixture back into the ice cream container. Smooth the top and cover with plastic wrap. Freeze overnight.

OPTIONAL: Serve sprinkled with more marshmallows and shaved chocolate.

Vanilla Ice Cream

SERVES 6 TO 8

A terrific little recipe by the gorgeous Carly Nelson.

2½ cups heavy cream, lightly whipped

3 cups whole milk

2 tablespoons vanilla extract

1½ cups sugar

Mix all the ingredients together until thoroughly combined. Place in the freezer for at least 4 hours prior to serving. Easy and cheap!

OPTIONAL: Mix in some flaked chocolate or fresh fruit for variety—everyone will love it!

GLUTEN-FREE LUNCH BOXES

To bring up a child in the way he should go,
travel that way yourself once in a while.
—Josh Billings

We are mothers with little boys who eat and eat and eat! When it comes to lunch boxes, sometimes it's hard enough trying to find a balance between good nutrition and foods the kids will eat. Add to that gluten-free options, and you have yourself quite a challenge!!!

There are lots of ways to pack a healthy, gluten-free school lunch. Start by getting your children involved in the weekly menu planning process. This generally increases the odds that they will actually eat what you pack for them!

According to The Coeliac Society of Australia's December 2008 newsletter, a lunch box should always include:

- At least 2 pieces of fruit or vegetables (fresh, dried, or canned)
- At least 1 serving of dairy, such as yogurt, milk, or cheese
- At least 3 or 4 servings of carbohydrate-rich foods, such as bread, crackers, grain- and fruit-based bars, pasta, etc.
- At least 1 serving of protein

The recommended servings from each food group vary with age. If you are unsure what your child requires, you may want to seek advice from your pediatrician or a dietitian.

Here are twenty-five of our favorite suggestions of what to include in a lunch box, gathered from far and wide.

1. To avoid waste, use your leftovers in many of the following ideas and options.
2. Fruit: Make it easier to eat. Peel oranges or cut a kiwifruit in half, and include a spoon in the lunch box.

3. Fruit kebabs: Pineapple, honeydew, apple, grapes, oranges, and strawberries are all great cubed and threaded onto a skewer.

4. Fruit pieces with yogurt to dip into (add a dash of cinnamon to the yogurt).

5. Dried fruit: In season, dry your own mango; the children will love it!

6. Banana chips lightly dipped in chocolate.

7. Vegetables: Raw vegetables cut into slices or florets are fabulous as dipping sticks for your child's favorite dip. Our children love the Avo & Corn Dip (page 3).

8. Celery sticks stuffed with peanut butter and sprinkled with raisins. Or if peanut butter is a no-go, try cottage cheese.

9. Cheese cubes served with your favorite GF crackers, rice crackers, or GF pretzels.

10. Pancakes can be naturally sweetened with the zest of an orange.

11. Plain popcorn (add a small amount of dried fruit for variety).

12. Cinnamon popcorn: This is delish! In a small saucepan, melt 2 tablespoons butter. Then add 1 tablespoon brown sugar and ½ teaspoon cinnamon, drizzle over a bowl of plain popped popcorn, and toss to mix.

13. Creamy rice with fruit.

14. GF pita bread.

15. Homemade tortilla chips: Cut tortillas into triangles, sprinkle with a little Parmesan, and bake at 350°F for 15 to 20 minutes, or until crisp.

16. GF sausages cut into bite-size pieces.

17. Chicken drumsticks.

18. Fish cakes made with canned tuna or salmon, egg, potato, and peas are yummy!

19. Corn tortillas for roll-up sandwiches: ham, cheese, and shredded lettuce; or hummus, cheese, and thinly sliced tomato.

20. Corn tortillas for pizza bases:
    Margherita: Pizza sauce, fresh basil, and mozzarella
    Hawaiian: Pizza sauce, GF ham, pineapple, and mozzarella
    Pepperoni: Pizza sauce, GF pepperoni, and mozzarella
    Italian: Pizza sauce, olives, GF salami, and mozzarella
    Mexican: Salsa, avocado, sour cream, and mozzarella
21. GF corn chips with guacamole (which can be as simple as a mashed avocado with a dollop of salsa and a dollop of sour cream).
22. Lettuce wraps: Fill an iceberg lettuce leaf with GF shredded ham and grated cheese and gently roll it. Wrap it with a chive or seal it with a toothpick to hold it together.
23. Parmesan Crisps (page 47): Your children will looooove these served with their favorite dips.
24. Almond Muffins (page 29): Add a variety of fruit to the mix to vary the flavor.
25. Chocolate Balls (page 221): Our little boys looooooooooooooooove it when these turn up by surprise in their lunch boxes. These freeze well, too, so make a bunch!!!

Gluten-free need not be taste-free!
—The Coeliac Society of Australia

FOR THE BABY
& TODDLERS

A baby will make love stronger
Days shorter, nights longer
Bankroll smaller
Home happier, clothes shabbier
The past forgotten
And the future worth living for.

—Anonymous

Bananavo

Recipe by Kim Morrison. This is tops!

¼ avocado
¼ banana

Mash and combine well together and serve.

Brazilian Fried Bananas

1 tablespoon butter
1 banana, thickly sliced
1 tablespoon cinnamon sugar

In a small skillet, melt the butter over medium heat. Add the banana slices and cook until just starting to toast, then turn and cook until both sides are golden brown. Sprinkle with the cinnamon sugar and let it caramelize. Remove from the pan and serve warm.

OPTIONAL: These are delish served drizzled with Egg Custard (page 224).

Broccoli & Cheddar Nuggets

½ head broccoli, cut into small pieces

½ cup GF seasoned bread crumbs

½ cup grated Cheddar cheese

3 egg yolks (or 2 whole eggs if baby is over a year old)

Preheat the oven to 350°F. Line a baking sheet with parchment paper. In a large bowl, mix all the ingredients together and form into nuggetlike shapes. Place on the baking sheet and bake for 25 minutes, turning after 15 minutes. Serve warm.

Caramel Milk

2 cups whole milk

5 tablespoons light brown sugar

¼ teaspoon vanilla extract

In a saucepan, heat the milk over medium heat. Stir in the brown sugar and vanilla and serve warm.

Cheesy Frittata

1 large potato, peeled and thinly sliced

1 tablespoon butter

3 eggs, lightly beaten

½ cup grated Cheddar cheese

In a saucepan of boiling water, cook the potato until tender. Drain. In a nonstick skillet, heat the butter over medium heat. Layer in the potatoes. Pour the eggs over the potatoes, sprinkle with the Cheddar, and cook until bubbles begin to appear on the surface. Flip when golden and cook the underside. Cut into wedges to serve.

Creamy Rice

2 cups short-grain rice

2 cups whole milk

1 teaspoon grated nutmeg

In a saucepan, bring 2 cups water to a boil. Add the rice and cook until the water is absorbed. Add the milk and return to a boil. Reduce the heat to a simmer and cook, stirring regularly, for 15 minutes, or until the rice is tender. Let cool and serve sprinkled with nutmeg.

French Toast

Serve with a drizzle of jam or honey if your child is more than one year old.

1 egg

1 tablespoon milk

2 slices GF bread, crusts removed

1 teaspoon butter

In a shallow dish, beat the egg and milk until well blended. Cut each slice of bread into thirds. In a nonstick skillet, heat the butter. Dip the bread into the egg mixture, coating both sides well. Add the bread to the skillet and cook on both sides until golden brown.

NOTE: This is a great way to use up stale bread!

Pureed Apple & Cinnamon

1 apple, peeled and
chopped

½ teaspoon cinnamon sugar

In a small saucepan, combine the apple with water to cover. Bring to a boil and simmer until soft. Pour off any excess liquid, add the cinnamon sugar, and mash.

Sweet Potato Fries

1 sweet potato, peeled and
cut into small wedges

2 tablespoons olive oil

1 teaspoon cinnamon sugar

Preheat the oven to 350°F. Line a baking sheet with parchment paper. In a plastic bag, combine the sweet potato and oil and shake until the wedges are coated. Arrange on the baking sheet and sprinkle with the cinnamon sugar. Turn to coat all sides; then bake for 20 to 30 minutes, depending on thickness, or until tender. Serve warm.

Tofu Nuggets

¼ cup GF all-purpose flour

1 teaspoon garlic powder

1 package (12 ounces) firm tofu

1 egg yolk, beaten

Preheat the oven to 350°F. Combine the flour, garlic powder, and a little pepper. Cut the tofu into cubes or fingers manageable for your baby or toddler. Roll in the egg yolk, coating well, then dredge in the seasoned flour. Chill in the fridge for 5 minutes before baking for 15 minutes.

OPTIONAL: Add some GF bread crumbs to the seasoned flour for a little crunch.

NOTE: Frozen bread grates more easily.

Veggie Fruit Mash

Flynn Turnbull's favorite.

1 Granny Smith apple, peeled and chopped

8 ounces sweet potato, peeled and chopped

Kernels from 1 ear of corn

6 plump blueberries

In a saucepan, combine the apple, sweet potato, corn, and 1½ cups water and bring to a boil. Cook until tender. Transfer to a blender, add the blueberries, and puree. Serve warm.

HERBS TO THE RESCUE

The greatest sweetener of human life is friendship.
—Anonymous

Whether you are cooking a meal with four or forty ingredients, you want it to be flavorsome! If you are taking the time to cook, you want it to be terrific!

What we have found in cooking with just four or fewer ingredients is that it is imperative for one of those ingredients to have a strong, dramatic flavor. This can easily be achieved simply by adding a fresh herb.

Here is a list of the herbs we have found most useful and what they complement. We hope you find them useful, too!!!

Basil: Basil is a perfect complement to tomatoes and it features heavily in Italian cuisine. It also works beautifully with cheese, pasta, eggs, meat, salads, soups, and casseroles. It is best torn, not cut, and added to dishes just before serving, as cooking diminishes its flavor.

Chives: These are the baby of the onion family. Chives give a great boost to the flavor of salads, potatoes, soups, sandwiches, dips, dressings, and mayonnaise and are best added just before serving. Use chives to rub on meat or seafood before grilling.

Cilantro: Cilantro is a fabulous accompaniment to most things Asian, especially Thai and Indian. It has a particular affinity for chicken, fish, curries, stir-fries, chutneys, and salads.

Dill: Dill leaves are used as an herb, but the seeds of the plant are used as a spice. Dill leaves (or dill weed) go well with seafood, chicken, beets, cucumber, many vegetable dishes, eggs, and vinegar.

Mint: If you haven't got an herb garden, start with mint, as it is the most difficult of all herbs to kill! It has a fresh, crisp flavor and is fabulous in salads, or with seafood, lamb, peas, potatoes, yogurt, fresh berries, and fresh pineapple. Or break off a sprig and pop it into a fruit punch or a jug of water with ice. Use it to garnish desserts, especially chocolate ones.

Oregano: Also known as wild marjoram, oregano is widely used in Italian cooking and is perfect in pastas and sprinkled on pizzas. Additionally, it complements pork, chicken, eggplant, pepper, olives, zucchini, and sauces.

Parsley: The world's most popular herb! Like most fresh herbs, it is high in vitamins and minerals and adds a delicious flavor to garlic, eggs, vegetables, cheese and potato dishes, fish, soups, and poultry. Use it as a garnish, or sprinkle it over salads and pizzas just before serving to add a healthy, fresh taste.

Tarragon: This herb adds a unique zing to seafood, chicken, lamb, tomato, and sauces! Did you know that béarnaise sauce is just hollandaise with tarragon?

Thyme: This is one of our personal favorites. We wish we had more of it! It is absolutely spectacular in our Baked Ricotta & Thyme Pie (page 155) and our Sautéed Cherry Tomatoes (page 99). It imparts a fabulous flavor to all kinds of red-meat dishes, soups, sauces, and vegetable dishes. It also provides a tasty stuffing for chicken.

OILS EXPLAINED

I stand in front of the oil aisle at my local supermarket
with literally hundreds of bottles looking back at me and I wonder to myself,
what is the difference????
—Confused Shopper

Many of the following oils are used in *4 Ingredients Gluten-Free*. Our research and questions unearthed the following information.

Avocado Oil: This oil is made from pressing the flesh of avocados. It complements seafood and salads and can be drizzled over roasts prior to baking. It is sensational in the place of peanut or sesame oil in salads.

Grapeseed Oil: A vegetable oil pressed from the seeds of several varieties of *Vitis vinifera* grapes, an abundant by-product of winemaking. This oil is fabulous in salad dressings and also in barbecue marinades, as it has a very unobtrusive flavor.

Macadamia Oil: Macadamia oil is cold-pressed from the nuts of the macadamia tree. Macadamia oil is the crème de la crème of nut oils. It is an excellent frying oil due to its high ignition point, and it is loaded with nutrients.

Olive Oil: Olive oil comes in varying grades from extra virgin to a blended mix found in most supermarkets. To explain the difference, it is interesting to note how the oil is produced.

    1st step. Olives are picked, sorted, and washed.

    2nd step. They are placed in a press to extract the oil. This is known as the first, or "virgin," press and gives rise to what we call extra virgin olive oil. When buying, look for the words "first cold pressed" on the label to be sure you are buying the correct oil. This oil is the best to buy, as it hasn't been heated and is therefore still loaded with flavor and nutrients. It is best used in salads or at the very end of a cooking process.

3rd step. A second press produces virgin olive oil. During this process the oil is slightly heated, thereby losing some of its nutrients and flavor. Virgin olive oil is best used in most types of cooking except frying, as its smoke point (the point where it will catch fire) is relatively low.

4th step. The third press process produces what is labeled simply olive oil. This oil is best used in all general cooking.

Sesame Oil: This is naturally obtained from sesame seeds. It is a very flavorful oil and should be used sparingly as a dressing for salads and in stir-fries. It is best to use only a small amount due to its low smoke point, to ensure that the oil doesn't ignite.

Sunflower Oil: Ideal for use as a general cooking oil and, because of its very mild taste, at those times when you don't want a strong, intrusive flavor, such as when you are making mayonnaise, baking cakes, and frying.

Walnut Oil: With a delicate, nutty flavor, this oil is perfect in a salad dressing, drizzled over steamed vegetables, as a flavoring for fish or steak, or for use in baking.

HANDY HOME TIPS

Dream . . . Believe . . . Create.
—Jennette McCosker, Bella Boo Cafe, 2008

Aching feet and chest colds: Apply a thick coat of chest rub and cover feet with a pair of socks before going to bed at night.

Baby wipes: Are great for brightening kids' white leather shoes.

Basil oil: To make basil oil, soak basil leaves in a jar of olive oil. Yummy drizzled over salads or used in frying meats, cheeses, etc.

Bathroom odors: Place an opened box of baking soda or an open container of activated charcoal behind the toilet to absorb bathroom odors.

Broken glass: Pick up small shards of glass that remain after you've cleared the big pieces by blotting the area with wet newspapers. The tiny fragments will stick to the paper.

Bubble gum in hair: To remove, simply rub some peanut butter onto the gummed hair. You will need to wash the hair afterward, but the peanut butter helps the gum slide off.

Butter: For softened butter in a hurry, grate it. It works a treat.

Cake pans: Use some of the dry ingredients from the cake recipe to "flour" a cake pan, instead of flour. No white flour smudges on the outside of the cake!

Candleholders: To prevent the melting wax from sticking to the inside of a votive candleholder, pour a bit of water into the holder, then place the candle on top. If you're reading this tip too late, and there's already wax stuck inside your candleholder, pop it into the freezer for an hour. The wax will chip right off.

Candle wax: To remove wax from carpeting or other fabric, first scrape away any excess. Then place a brown paper bag over the wax and run a warm iron over the bag. The wax will melt right into the bag! Continue moving the bag around as you pick up the wax so you are always using a clean section. If a little grease stain remains on the carpet, sprinkle with baking soda and allow to sit overnight before vacuuming, which will remove the grease residue. If colored wax leaves a stain on the carpet, blot with spot remover or carpet cleaner, following the label directions.

CDs: Repair scratched CDs by rubbing with smooth peanut butter and wiping it off with a coffee filter.

Clothespins: Use a clothespin to hold nails in place when hammering in hard-to-reach places.

Coffee and tea stains: Remove coffee and tea stains from rugs by pouring a little beer over the stain. Lightly rub the beer into the material, and the stain should disappear. You may have to do it a couple of times to remove all stains.

Coffee filter: A paper coffee filter is microwave safe and makes a great cover over food to prevent splattering when cooking in the microwave.

Coffee mugs: Clean coffee-stained mugs by rinsing out, then rubbing with salt. Leave for approximately 5 minutes before rinsing. Stains should be removed, but you may have to repeat.

Cold compress: Keep a cold compress on hand by rinsing a washcloth in cold water. While still wet, place it in a ziplock bag and freeze. Next time you need a cold compress just wrap in a kitchen towel and apply.

Computer keyboards: Clean computer keyboards with nail polish remover and an old toothbrush. Simply moisten the brush with remover and lightly rub the keys.

Cookbooks: Keep cookbooks free of splatters when cooking by placing them in a clear plastic bag.

Crayon on walls or washable wallpaper: Spray with WD-40, then gently wipe, using a paper towel or clean cloth. If the mark is stubborn, sprinkle a little baking soda on a damp sponge and gently rub in a circular motion. If the WD-40 leaves a residue, gently wipe off with a sponge soaked in soapy water; rinse clean; blot dry. Another method is to use a hair dryer—it heats the wax so it wipes away instantly. If the color remains, as red usually does, wet a cloth with bleach and wipe. Or use baby oil! Red crayon may be a little more stubborn, but one wipe is usually all it takes!

Dryer tip: Include a few tennis balls in each dryer cycle. The tennis balls not only cut drying time by 25 to 50 percent, but also fluff the clothes to a delicate softness. Towels will be especially fluffy.

Dusting and polishing: Oven mitts are great for dusting and polishing furniture. Use one side of the mitt to apply wax or polish to your furniture and the other side to buff it up. Wash afterward to use again and again.

Fatigue: Drink a glass of grapefruit and lemon juice in equal parts to dispel fatigue and general tiredness after a day's work.

Fresh flowers: To keep cut flowers from sagging in their vase, crisscross several pieces of transparent tape across the mouth of the vase, leaving spaces where you can insert the flowers. The flowers will look perky and fresh for a few extra days.

Hair conditioner: Use to protect your shoes during winter. Lather your shoes or boots with conditioner. It is also a good leather conditioner.

Hair dye: Run a bit of Vaseline across your hairline to stop hair dye from staining your skin.

Hangover: Eat honey on GF crackers. The fructose in the honey will help to flush out the alcohol in your system.

Headache: Eat 10 to 12 almonds, the equivalent of two aspirins, for a migraine headache. Almonds are far less likely to upset the stomach.

Ink stains: Remove ink stains by rubbing alcohol on the stain before washing.

Insect bites: Mix water with cornstarch to form a paste, and apply. This is effective in drawing out the poisons of most insect bites and is also an effective remedy for diaper rash. Calendula oil also works brilliantly.

Ironing: Add a drop of your favorite essential oil to the water in your iron to give your clothes a lovely fragrance. And if you are ironing delicates, there's no need to adjust the heat settings. Just cover with parchment paper and iron.

Jewelry: Give jewelry a great sparkle by placing it in a glass of warm water, dropping in an Alka-Seltzer tablet, and letting it soak for a couple of minutes. Polish with a soft cloth.

Kids' artwork: If you want to save some of your kids' precious artwork, simply roll up the artwork and place inside a paper towel tube. Label the outside with the child's name and date.

Kitty litter: To keep cat litter smelling fresh, mix baby powder in with the litter.

Lipstick stains: Get rid of lipstick stains from cloth napkins by dabbing with Vaseline before popping into the washing machine.

Microwave cleaning: Food splatters all over the inside of your microwave and cooks itself on over time. To easily remove this mess, place a sponge soaked in water in the microwave. Cook on high heat for 2 minutes, then let sit without opening the microwave door for 5 minutes. The filth is now ready to be wiped right off—no scrubbing—and your sponge is right there!

Milk cartons: Slice the top off a half-gallon or gallon milk carton. Fill with food scraps for the compost heap.

Mosquito bites: With a cotton ball, apply lime juice diluted with water on bites.

Mothball substitute: Take your leftover soap slivers and put them in a vented plastic bag. Place the bag with seasonal clothes before packing them away. Not only will the scent prevent them from moth harm, but they'll smell great when you pull them out.

Nail polish: Keep nail polish fresh and easy to use by storing in the refrigerator.

Odd socks: Save on purchasing sponges for your car. Slip an odd sock over your hand and use as a cleaning mitt with your normal car wash detergent.

Oil stains on concrete: Remove unsightly grease, oil, and transmission fluid stains from your concrete driveway or garage floor by spraying with oven cleaner. Let settle for 5 to 10 minutes, then scrub with a stiff brush and rinse.

Paintbrushes: When taking a break from painting, wrap brushes in plastic wrap. They will stay moist and wet for a couple of hours.

Pillowcases: Use pillowcases to keep linen sets together. Use one pillowcase and fold up and place inside it both sheets and the other pillowcase. No more searching for matching pieces!

Potatoes: Stop potatoes from budding by storing an apple with them.

Red wine stains: To remove red wine stains from carpet, while the stain is still wet, pour on some white wine to dilute the color, then clean with a sponge and cold water. Sprinkle the area with salt and wait 10 minutes before vacuuming up the mess.

Repel insects: Dilute 1 tablespoon vanilla extract in 1 cup water and wipe the mixture on any exposed skin to discourage mosquitoes, bush flies, and ticks.

Scissors: To sharpen old scissors, use them to cut up a sheet of aluminum foil. The more you cut, the sharper the scissors become.

Shaving cuts: Dab a bit of lip balm directly onto the nick, and the bleeding from most shaving cuts will quickly stop.

Smelly feet: Soak feet in strong tea for 20 minutes every day until the smell disappears. To prepare your footbath, brew 2 tea bags in 2½ cups of water for 15 minutes and pour the tea into a basin containing 2 quarts of cool water.

Sore throat: Mix 1 teaspoon lime juice and 1 tablespoon honey. Swallow tiny amounts slowly 2 to 3 times a day.

Speed-dry nail polish: Spray painted nails with a coat of olive oil cooking spray and let it dry. The spray is also a great moisturizer for your hands.

Spilled eggs: Clean up spilled uncooked egg by sprinkling with salt. It will draw the egg together and you can easily wipe it up with a sponge or paper towel.

Splinters: Lay Scotch tape over the splinter and pull off, or soak the area in vegetable oil for a few minutes before removing the splinter with tweezers.

Stain removers: Reach for baby wipes anytime you notice something on your clothes or the kids' clothes—you'll see it gone in no time. We don't know what is in them, but they work a treat.

Stickers, decals, and glue: To remove them from furniture, glass, plastic, etc., saturate with vegetable oil and rub off.

Wite-Out/Liquid Paper and permanent marker stains: Dab some sunscreen over the stain and rub off with a paper towel. Repeat until the stain is gone.

Zippers: To make a zipper slide up and down more smoothly, rub a bar of soap over the teeth.

BIBLIOGRAPHY

Coppedge, Richard J., Jr., C.M.B. *Gluten-Free Baking with The Culinary Institute of America*. Avon, Mass.: Adams Media, 2008.

Heaton, Nell. *Cookery To-day and To-morrow*. London: The Syndicate Publishing Co., Ltd., 1946.

Hillis, Anne, and Penelope Stone. *Breast Bottle Bowl*. Pymble, Sydney, N.S.W.: HarperCollins Publishers, 1993.

Korn, Danna. *Living Gluten-Free for Dummies*. Hoboken, N.J.: Wiley Publishing, Inc., 2006.

Lai, Oneka. Popular Rice Dishes. Waterloo, N.S.W.: Australian Universities Press, 1973.

Magazine of the Coeliac Society of Australia, December 2008. Waitera, N.S.W.: The Coeliac Society of Australia.

O'Meara, Cyndi. *Changing Habits, Changing Lives*. Victoria, Australia: Penguin Books, 2000.

———. *Changing Habits, Changing Lives Cookbook*. Victoria, Australia, 2002.

Take 5 Top Tips. ACP magazines, a division of ACP PBL Media Pty Ltd. ACP Magazines Ltd., 2009.

Tortilla International. Santa Rosa, Calif.: Cole Group, Inc., 1995.

Whitby, Joanna. *Practical Cooking for Babies and Toddlers*. Marrickville, N.S.W.: Choice Books, 1999.

Websites

What is Coeliac Disease?
www.coeliacsociety.com.au/
www.coeliacresearchfund.org

Gluten-Free Diets
www.gastro.net.au/diets/glutenfree.html

Gluten Free and Easy
www.glutenfreeandeasy.com/Active/ingredients.html

Coeliac Resources
www.basco.com.au/

Recipes and Tips
www.basicingredients.com.au/GF.html

Gluten-Free Foods
www.glutenfreedirect.com.au/
www.glutenfreegoodies.com.au

How to Pack a Healthy Gluten-Free School Lunch for Your Gluten-Free Child
http://glutenfreecooking.about.com/od/glutenfreekids/ht/gflunchboxtips.htm

Gluten Free Gobsmacked
http://glutenfree.wordpress.com/2008/08/21/gluten-free-lunch-to-go-ideas-for-what-to-pack/

All I Really Need to Know I Learned in Kindergarten
www.robertfulghum.com

Finger food ideas for making homemade baby food
www.wholesomebabyfood.com/content/babyfoodFingerFoods.pdf

Herbs Explained by Jenelle Johnson
www.iolaregister.com/Local%20News/Stories/Herbsexplained.html

Herbs and Spices
www.gourmetgarden.com/au/

The essential guide to oils
http://recipefinder.ninemsn.com.au/article.aspx?id=281737

INDEX

ABOUT THE AUTHORS

Rachael Bermingham is the energetic, dynamic, and proud mum to Jaxson and twin boys Bowie and Casey. She has written six bestselling books in the last five years and is regarded as one of Australia's leading female authors. Rachael wrote two bestselling books, *Read My Lips* and *How to Write Your Own Book and Make It a Bestseller*, before writing the phenomenally successful *4 Ingredients* cookbooks with her dear friend Kim McCosker. She travels the world as a motivational speaker and mentor and is the founder of Bermingham Books, a mentoring and book distribution center for authors wanting to know how to write, produce, and promote their own books.

When Rachael's not working or whipping up something fabulous in the kitchen, she can be found "chillaxing" at home with friends and family and soaking up the sun, surf, and sand of the beautiful Sunshine Coast in Australia. Find out more at www.rachaelbermingham.com or email her at Rachael@4ingredients.com.au.

Kim McCosker is the proud mother of three boys (Morgan, nine; Hamilton, six; and Flynn, three) and the coauthor of the internationally bestselling 4 Ingredients series, which includes *4 Ingredients* and *4 Ingredients Gluten-Free*. She recently received the Outstanding Business Woman of the Year Award from the Sunshine Coast Business Women's Network.

For Kim, family is the most important thing in the world, and with the loving support of her wonderful husband, Glen, she has been able to juggle the demands of a busy work life and her treasured home life. Life presents many opportunities, but having the courage and the time to pursue them in what is an increasingly busy and demanding world is hard. She is living proof that you can achieve whatever you want with a great idea and lots of hard work! Write to her at info@4ingredients.com.au.

Go to www.4ingredientss.com.au or www.facebook.com/4ingredients to find out more.

INVITATION

Join Our Foodie Family!

AT 4 INGREDIENTS we cultivate a family of busy people all bound together by the desire to create good, healthy, home-made meals quickly, easily, and economically. Our aim is to save us all precious time and money in the kitchen. If this is you, too, then we invite you to join our growing family, where we share kitchen wisdom daily. If you have a favorite recipe or a tip that has worked for you in your kitchen and think others would enjoy it, please join our family at:

f facebook.com/4ingredientspage

You Tube 4 Ingredients Channel

www 4ingredients.com.au

@4ingredients

Happy Cooking!

Kim & Rachael